Back to the Drawing Board

DESIGNING CORPORATE BOARDS
FOR A COMPLEX WORLD

Back to the Drawing Board

Colin B. Carter
and Jay W. Lorsch

HARVARD BUSINESS SCHOOL PRESS

Boston, Massachusetts

Copyright 2004 Harvard Business School Publishing Corporation

Library of Congress Cataloging-in-Publication Data
    Carter, Colin B.
    Back to the drawing board : designing corporate boards for a complex world /
    Colin B. Carter and Jay W. Lorsch.
        p. cm.
    Includes bibliographical references and index.
    ISBN 1-57851-776-1 (alk. paper)
        1. Directors of corporations   2. Corporate governance.   I. Lorsch, Jay William.
    II. Title.
    HD2745.C365 2004
    658.4'22—dc21

                                                            2003009334

The paper used in this publication meets the requirements of the American National
Standard for Permanence of Paper for Publications and Documents in Libraries and
Archives Z39.48-1992.

To Angie
C. B. C.

To Patricia
J. W. L.

Contents

Preface

Our collaboration began in 1999 when we first sat down to share our separate experiences working with boards. From this initial conversation grew the idea to create this book, and it's truly the result of an equal effort between a consultant and a professor. During the intervening years we have continued to work separately as board members and as consultants to boards and have had numerous conversations together about our experiences and about the ideas that are articulated in the following pages.

As we were in the midst of committing our ideas to our computers in 2001 with chapters being e-mailed halfway around the world, the corporate governance scandals and excesses were revealed in North America and elsewhere. For us the fact that boards were culpable for some of these problems was an unexpected opportunity. Our position from the start was that while boards had been improving in many countries over the previous decade, too many were still unable to carry out their mandate effectively. As we began to write, we believed our initial task would be to convince readers of these facts. After Enron, Tyco, World-Com, et al., we suddenly faced a new challenge. We had to balance two conflicting facts—that while some boards could be blamed for aspects of these corporate governance failures, at the same time other boards were actually improving their functioning. This is a central theme of this book, but an equally important corollary is that in the future boards will face even more challenges with inadequate resources to meet them. For each board to accomplish what is expected of it, now and in the future, will require a fundamental reexamination of its role and "redesign" of its structure and processes.

The many hundreds of directors and senior executives to whom we have spoken over the past years cannot be named. Many have been on the boards we have worked with as consultants. Others have been participants in educational programs for directors at Harvard Business School. We are particularly grateful to those chairmen and directors who have asked us to review the performance of their boards and, in so doing, given us license to explore what really goes on behind closed boardroom doors. Others who have helped us are codirectors on boards on which we serve or simply friends and professional colleagues with whom we have spent many hours discussing and refining our views. Their contribution has been substantial and we hope that they see some of their insights reflected in this final product.

This book has been a collaboration not only between the two of us, but also among many colleagues and clients who have helped us as we have formed the ideas and approaches described in this book. They have been generous with their time, experience, and insights. In particular, we thank our colleagues at The Boston Consulting Group (BCG) and Harvard Business School (HBS) who have tested our ideas and provided the resources to support this work.

We especially want to recognize several of Colin's colleagues at BCG. Mark Blaxill introduced us to each other on the surmise that we might write a book together about boards and he has been proven correct. Carl Stern, Tom Lewis, Mark Joiner, Alan Jackson, and Bolko von Oetinger have provided financial support as well as unlimited encouragement to complete this project. Others, including René Abate, Robert Howard, Lars Terney, Peter Goldsbrough, Ted Buswick, Sandy Moose, George Pappas, and Maurie Koop, commented on drafts and helped to debate the ideas; Rick Wright helped with analysis; and Yvonne White provided valuable editorial input on early drafts. A number of the BCG partners introduced our research questionnaire to their CEO clients and this enabled us to gain a view of boards from this important group of senior executives. We also appreciate the time these busy executives have taken to complete the questionnaire.

At HBS we wish to thank Jay's colleagues with whom we have discussed these ideas. This especially includes those involved in the Global Corporate Governance Initiative, Dwight Crane, Alexander Dyck, Brian Hall, Paul Healy, Carl Kester, Rakesh Khurana, and Krishna Palepu. The members of the Initiative's Advisory Council have also provided helpful insight. We want to recognize, in particular, Helmut Sihler and Daniel Vasella, who gave us access to and insight about European boards. The work of the Global Initiative has been supported by a grant from Russell Reynolds Associates and we thank the partners of that firm for their generosity.

We also wish to thank the Harvard Business School Division of Research for its financial support and Dean Kim Clark for his support and encouragement of this work and also the faculty's broader research and teaching agenda related to corporate governance.

There is an old adage that the best way to learn is to teach and we would be remiss if we did not also express our gratitude to the M.B.A. students in Jay's course—The Board of Directors and Corporate Governance. They have been unwitting and intelligent participants in discussions that also shaped some of our ideas. As they learned from class discussions, so did we.

At HBS we also want to thank three research associates who were immensely helpful in various stages of our research—Katharina Pick, Sonya Sanchez, and Andy Zelleke.

Our own personal assistants have been an enormous help to us and without them this book would still be a work-in-process—coordinating and facilitating collaboration across so many time zones and thousands of miles was not easy. We are immensely grateful to Jane Barrett at HBS and Ipek Gyi at BCG. They helped us to ensure that the various drafts were kept under control and complete, and in many other ways we cannot recall.

Regina Maruca demonstrated her great editorial talent as she took our drafts and melded them into an end product that captured our thinking and was also readable. She did this admirably and without fuss. Her advice has been wise as she successfully synthesized our two voices and has sharpened our thinking.

We are also grateful to Jeff Kehoe, our editor at Harvard Business School Press, whose professional expertise and encouragement has been a major factor in getting this book finished. He saw the possibilities from the beginning and has offered wise counsel and editorial insight throughout.

Finally, we thank our families. Our wives, Patricia and Angie, have been very patient with our preoccupation with this project and given us the support that is required of partners when a book like this is being written! We also thank Patricia for her suggestion of *Back to the Drawing Board* as a title for this book. It captures our intent very nicely.

To all who have collaborated with us, knowingly and unknowingly, we are very grateful.

Boston and Melbourne

May 2003

Back to the
Drawing
Board

CHAPTER one

Board Design —
Time for Action

CONSIDER A BOARD OF DIRECTORS YOU KNOW WELL. You may be a member of that board, or an executive in the company it governs. Or you may be a shareholder. Do you believe that the board performs anywhere near to its potential? Are its members well informed about the important issues facing the company? Do they understand the industry in which they compete? Do they know what is driving the performance of the company, or the main risks it is taking? Are their responsibilities well defined? Is the board effective? Is it efficient? Chances are, your answers to most of those questions are "No," or "Not really." And chances are, your answers are negative *despite* the fact that this board has made an effort to improve itself within the past ten years.

Indeed, no board that we know of has been immune to recent reform initiatives. But most boards continue to struggle in spite of the increased scrutiny and regulatory reforms imposed from the outside, and the efforts many boards have pursued on their own. Directors continue to be overwhelmed by a slate of responsibilities that is only going to become more complex and difficult as time goes on.

Why hasn't all this effort resulted in more progress? We believe the answer, at its roots, is simple. Broadly speaking, the reforms we've seen to date do not identify or address the root cause of the problems most boards have: *inadequate attention to the way each board is designed to handle its responsibilities.*

Take the recommendations and reforms we've seen in the last two decades. In the United States, for example, beginning in the late 1980s, institutional investors like CalPers, the New York State Employee Retirement Fund, and later TIAA-CREF called for changes such as a greater proportion of independent directors, separating the job of board chairman and CEO, and limiting the number of boards on which a director should serve. During this time, the Securities and Exchange Commission also virtually required all boards of public companies to have a compensation committee made up of only independent directors.

More recently, in the wake of the corporate scandals in the United States during 2001 and 2002, even more pressure for change has developed. Most obvious is the Sarbanes-Oxley Act that, among other provisions, mandates that audit committees be made up of independent directors, and specifies their responsibilities in relation to the company's auditors.[1] The new listing requirements of the stock exchanges (NYSE, NASDAQ, and Amex) are also important; they put emphasis on the audit, compensation, and corporate governance committees of the board, as well as on independent directors and the importance of their meeting without management and with a leader other than the CEO.[2]

In the United Kingdom, consider the influential Cadbury Committee, established in 1991 under the sponsorship of the Financial Reporting Council, the London Stock Exchange, and the British accounting profession in response to concerns about the low level of investor confidence in financial reporting and in the ability of auditors to do their jobs. It may seem that Cadbury's focus should have been on recommendations for dealing with concerns about auditors and accounting and financial information, but instead, reacting to a spate of corporate scandals, the committee focused on boards in general, especially on separating the roles of chairman and CEO, and on establishing audit committees of the boards of all companies listed on the London Stock Exchange.[3] We mention the Cadbury example in large part because of the scope of its influence and also because it was the first significant reform effort in the United Kingdom in recent years. A host of other significant reports have since been published in the United Kingdom calling for board reform, among them most recently the Higgs Report on the role of non-executive directors and the Smith Report on audit committees.[4] Similar reform efforts have occurred in other European countries, including for example, France and the Netherlands.

Inside boardrooms, many directors have concluded that the best course of action is to spearhead their own reform efforts. Their concern being that if boards don't reform the way they function, they could face regulations and court decisions that would require even more drastic changes. The much-criticized board of General Motors (GM) in the early 1990s was very visible in this movement, publishing and publicizing its own set of governance guidelines.[5] An avalanche of similar statements from other major public corporations in the United States followed, and continues to this day.

All this effort has not been wasted. The various cries for reform in the boardroom, and the regulations, policies, and internal initiatives that have ensued, have led to a set of "best practices" that pointed many boards in the right direction in the 1990s. But none of these initiatives has brought about sustained effective action overall, for several reasons.

One is that most of the recommendations for change coming from external groups focus only on those characteristics of boards that are visible to outsiders. They say little about what should actually happen *inside* the boardroom, and as a result have too little substantive effect on governance.

Another is that each board's responsibilities are becoming more challenging and time-consuming. External expectations about what boards should be held accountable for are rising. Board responsibilities, which reflect those expectations as well as the requirements of reforms already in place, are ever greater. The result is that the gap between what directors do and what is expected of them—even on boards that have adopted these best practices—continues to grow.

There are also unresolved contradictions in board design that have never been acknowledged either internally or by reforms sought from outside the boardroom. For example, the truly independent board, which is in many ways desirable, will struggle to achieve an adequate understanding of its company's business. How boards should deal with such contradictions and other design problems is not yet on either their own radars or the broader governance agenda.

What's more, the discussion that results from periodic high-profile corporate scandals and corporate collapses, as important as it is, regularly sidetracks any meaningful progress on these more critical issues. By focusing attention on corporate wrongdoing and incompetence, the fact that even honest and diligent boards struggle to do their job is largely missed. Instead, the scandals feed a widely held belief that board members are frequently asleep at the wheel, or even captive to the management they are supposed to oversee. It is hardly surprising that investors, analysts, and regulators inevitably focus on the directors of a company when they're looking for someone to blame, because boards—whether they are labeled boards of directors or supervisory boards—are at the center of any corporate governance system. But the result is that the energy for reform is mostly directed at problems that are only the tip of the iceberg.

Further "patching"—layering more regulations, policies, and requirements on top of what already exists—will only make the situation worse. What's needed instead is a thorough board-by-board overhaul of design and practice. Boards need to go back to the drawing board. Faced with a difficult task and an even greater weight of expectations, each board will have to carefully define its own objectives and make a plan for how it can best carry them out.

Boards, in other words, need to consider explicitly what their roles should be in light of the circumstances of their companies; be clear about their limitations and constantly evaluate their progress; tackle head-on the complex issues of their structures, skills, and memberships; continuously rethink their complicated relationship with management; and strive to discover better ways of gathering and sharing the knowledge needed to carry out their tasks.

The answers will vary a great deal for each company because their circumstances differ. But let us be clear: In saying that each board will formulate its own unique set of solutions, we do not mean that directors can ignore the calls for reform and improvement that emanate from investors, stock exchanges, regulators, and legislators. Rather, we argue that there is ample room and an opportunity for each board, within established regulations, and with due consideration to current best practices, to design itself to be most effective in governing its company.

How to do that is the focus of this book.

Design Inside a Boardroom

A FEW COMPANIES have carefully thought about their board design. For example, in early 1999, J. T. Battenberg, Chairman and CEO of Delphi Corporation, had the unusual challenge of designing the board of directors for his newly independent and publicly owned company.[6] Delphi, which had formerly been a part of General Motors (GM), was the world's largest manufacturer of automobile components and transportation electronics. At the time of its public debut, it ranked fifty-seventh in revenues ($2.9 billion) on the list of *Fortune* 500 companies and employed nearly two hundred thousand people in forty countries around the globe.

One of the conditions of the spin-off was that only one GM director would join the Delphi board. Tom Wyman, a long-term board member, volunteered to join the Delphi board and to resign from the GM board to ensure the complete independence of Delphi from its former parent.

Battenberg welcomed Wyman's decision and asked him to serve as the board's lead director, which Wyman immediately agreed to do. Together they began to consider the new board's design. From the outset they agreed on three objectives. First, that the Delphi board would be designed so that it would avoid the problems of inaction and passivity that had plagued the GM board for so many years. As Wyman explained:

I was proud to serve on the GM board but we operated in a very passive manner. We were invited to join the board by the CEO, and rarely met alone to share our thoughts on the company's progress and, more particularly, on the performance of the CEO and management. The board endorsed annual plans and long-range strategies, but any role in developing or refining those plans was small. Board meetings were crowded with presentations, but with little time allotted for discussion. . . . Having a front row seat . . . at GM had a lasting impact on me and my work as lead director as Delphi's board was formed. We had an opportunity to decide not only what we wanted to be, but also what we didn't want to be. It's been a once-in-a-lifetime opportunity to build best practices into a board—opening with an empty blackboard.[7]

Their second goal was to use, as they deemed appropriate, the best fundamentals in board practices that had evolved in many U.S. boardrooms. Their third goal was to create a board that was appropriate for the circumstances Delphi faced. Uppermost in their minds was that Delphi had to establish its credibility with customers other than GM, and that these potential markets were not only in the United States but also in Asia, Europe, and Latin America. A second strategic imperative was controlling labor costs with a unionized work force. They also recognized that the new board would have to oversee a management and company heavily dependent on the development of new technology and products.

To achieve these goals, Battenberg and Wyman decided not only to create audit, compensation, and corporate governance committees, but to develop processes so the board would approve Delphi's strategic direction, provide feedback to Battenberg, monitor the company's progress, and assess the board's own performance. All of these were consistent with what they understood to be best practices. They also put emphasis on three unique requirements.

First, they selected directors who, while meeting the test of "independence," were knowledgeable about the automotive industry not just in the United States, but also globally. They wanted the wisdom and experience of these directors, as well as their help in meeting new potential customers. To meet this requirement, they selected one director from Europe, one from Japan, and one from Latin America.

Second, they wanted to develop a relationship between management and the board that would allow a free exchange of ideas and information in both directions. To achieve this they agreed that directors and management should talk freely with each other, without advising Battenberg about their conversations. They believed this would enable the board and management to work together constructively so that management could develop and implement, and the board could approve and assess, the company's strategy. Third, to further ensure that the board and management would work well together on strategy, they planned one annual three-day "strategic retreat" for the board and management, but equally important, they intended to keep the company's strategic direction on the agenda of all board meetings. In essence, they wanted a "rolling review" of company strategy.

The establishment of Delphi's board is a positive example of what can be accomplished when board members think carefully and consciously about what their board must accomplish and how best to organize themselves to do so. Unfortunately, when one looks at the landscape of boards in the major countries of the world, there are too few such positive examples of boards carefully considering their design.

The Case for Design

IT IS NOT SURPRISING that boards respond to the external pressures for change. But as we've said, our concern is that by focusing *only* on external pressures, boards are not exploring changes that will truly enable them to be more effective. As a result, most boards are a mixture of old and new practices, some of which conflict, and which do not together provide the best design to accomplish their growing responsibilities. There are vague notions of monitoring, of oversight, and of providing advice, or of being in on the big decisions, but no explicit attention is devoted to what role the board should play to meet its responsibilities.

It is also not surprising that boards rarely examine these fundamentals. A key reality for every board is that there is more to do than there is time to do it. Boards are so concerned with their month-to-month duties and getting through each meeting's agenda that it is extremely difficult for them to find the time to pause, stand back, and rethink their design. Yet in our judgment, this is exactly what boards must do if they are to meet the growing demands on them.

Think about it this way. Boards are like any other business organization, even though they are very small in membership and even though they sit at the pinnacle of the company hierarchy. If we were improving a factory or a sales organization, we would go back to basics and consider the mission of the unit and how to design an organization to make it more effective.

This is exactly what boards must do, and it is what we mean by "going back to the drawing board." Boards must go back to the basic questions, starting with their roles. What are their legal duties? On whose behalf are they governing? What do these parties want from their investment or other involvement in the company? In order to meet their obligations, what is the mix of activities in which boards should engage? What are the obstacles to doing the job right, and what resources are needed?

With this understanding of its role, each board can then consider the various elements in its design:

- The board structure—its size, leadership, and the committees it requires to accomplish its role
- The board composition—the mix of experience, skills, and other attributes of its members
- The board processes—how it gathers information, builds knowledge, and makes decisions

Structure, composition, and processes are the explicit design choices every board must make. These decisions are the "hard wiring"

FIGURE 1 - 1

The Board As a System

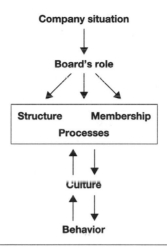

of the board's design and must be aligned to the role it intends to play and to the complexity of the company. These choices will also have an important impact on the behavior that occurs in the boardroom. And so boards must also consider what behaviors they wish to encourage or discourage, and make certain the board's design promotes the right behaviors. As this pattern of behavior persists, each board will develop its own unique culture that will itself further reinforce the behaviors found in that boardroom.

And so a board like any other organization is a *system* in which the behavior of the directors is shaped by the design elements and the board's culture (figure 1-1). The more effectively the elements in the board's design are aligned with each other and with the board's role, and the more deliberate the board is in defining the behaviors it wants to encourage, the more likely the system is to produce behaviors that will make the board effective.

Indeed, this is the scope and structure of our book. Our belief is that boards are struggling, and not even today's best practices are sufficient. Each board needs to be redesigned from the ground up, not in a piecemeal fashion, but by understanding itself as a system in which the elements should all be aligned.

We begin chapter 2 by describing how boards are struggling, notwithstanding the new best practices. In chapter 3 we examine the contradictions that are inherent even in the supposed best practices. Some are mutually inconsistent and others have unintended outcomes; all can seriously limit a board's capacity to do its job. The dilemmas they pose must be recognized and addressed in the design of a board if it is to be more effective.

The following chapters then outline the many ways in which a board can rethink its design. Chapter 4 focuses on how a board should conceive of its role. Today, conventional wisdom suggests that all boards should undertake very similar roles, but we believe that boards have considerable leeway in deciding what activities they wish to undertake, and that they must address this choice explicitly. Each board has to decide what it can and must accomplish, and different boards will legitimately reach very different answers.

Chapter 5 considers board structure—its size and leadership model, and what committees are needed and how they should be led and organized. These are the questions most susceptible to external governance pressure, because board structures can be observed from the outside and hence become the target for those who legitimately want boards to improve. We argue that too many of these propositions are accepted without critical assessment, and that structure is contextual. Like organization structures inside the company, the board's structures should be designed to fit its mission. There are broad principles to apply, but each board's structure must be aligned to its circumstances and intended role.

In chapter 6 we consider the critical question of selecting board members and enhancing their abilities—who should be on the board, how should they get there, and how can they be developed or removed? In the future, boards must think more carefully about how to select and develop a high-performance team.

Chapter 7 addresses a key problem for every board—designing a set of processes and practices so directors learn and stay better informed about their company and reach informed decisions. There is so much to learn and so little time to do it—which means that boards must explore innovative and sometimes controversial ways to build their knowledge. Directors will have to use technology, they will have to specialize, and they will have to widen their networks inside and outside their companies. The length and frequency of board meetings, as well as their agendas, processes, and meeting practices, will also have to change if directors are to make the most of their scarce time together.

In chapter 8 we focus on the behaviors that lead to effective boards. These will be shaped by the board's design. If the behavior in the boardroom is dysfunctional, it's a clear signal the board's design is flawed. "Bad" behavior occurs too frequently in too many boardrooms. Even very important people, late in their illustrious careers, can misbehave. In this chapter we also explore how boards can monitor and deal with such problems.

Finally, chapter 9 is a summary chapter in which we examine the effective board from a more personal perspective. We talk to the people sitting around the table about the part they must play in future improvements—the independent directors, the executive directors, and most important, the board leaders—the CEOs, chairmen, lead directors, and committee chairmen.

Further improvements in board effectiveness will mostly come from careful design. For some, such a design will lead to bold new directions.

A Global Perspective

I T I S O U R V I E W that the principles of board design on which this book focuses are appropriate to all companies in all countries. Board activism and empowerment had its origins in the English-speaking countries, such as Australia, Canada, the United Kingdom, and the United States, but as global capital flows have grown and as investor crises have unfolded in a number of other countries, pressures for improving corporate governance have become global. International institutions such as the World Bank, the Organisation for Economic Co-operation and Development (OECD), and the International Monetary Fund (IMF) have called for stronger institutions of corporate governance, emphasizing disclosure of information and protection of minority shareholders.[8] But demands to strengthen the governing boards have been at the core of all these calls for improvement.

Certainly there are differences in practice across countries. For example, Americans prefer combining the job of chairman and CEO, while Australians, the British, and most other Europeans prefer to separate them. On the other hand, U.S. and Australian boards have a much higher proportion of non-executives than British boards. U.S. boards have moved to pay their non-executive directors substantially in stock and options, while most other countries are slower to do this.

In spite of such differences, there has been an emerging consensus about how boards should function and be organized. This is not only becoming the accepted standard for boards in the English-speaking part of the world, but also the implicit model being recommended elsewhere as well.

Across Europe, there have been calls for improvement in corporate governance in general and in boards in particular. In the Netherlands, there was the Peters Report, sponsored by the Amsterdam Stock Exchange, calling for such changes.[9] Similarly, in France there have been two Vienot Reports—in 1995 and 1999—and most recently the Bouton Report in 2002.[10] In Germany there have been discussions among shareholders, business leaders, union officials, and politicians about the merits of their approach to corporate governance, and in 2002 a new code of corporate governance was promulgated calling for, among other things, more independent directors.[11]

In Australia, regulators as well as the stock exchange are stipulating tighter requirements for audit practice and board independence.[12] In Korea, the government has mandated the proportion of independent directors on a board, and many other countries are gradually moving to adopt similar standards.[13] In Japan, there have been a number of reports about the need for changes in boardrooms, although so far the adoption of new practices has been limited to a few companies, such as Sony.[14]

As we've said, we believe the principles on which we're basing this book are relevant and useful for all companies in all countries. Of course, there are countries with economic and political traditions and institutions and ownership situations different from the English-speaking countries. In these settings, boards must be designed to provide international investors the protection they seek while recognizing national differences. This means that one size will not fit all countries or companies, and that there is no universal template for the ideal board design. The need to build boards that recognize these differences but also meet standards acceptable to the global investor community is another strong argument for the explicit design of boards. Careful forethought will enable boards to meet both sets of requirements.

For these reasons, we are addressing directors around the world in this book. This orientation is consistent with our personal experience in serving on and consulting to boards. Between us we have experience with boards not only in the United States and Australia, but also in Asia, Europe, and Latin America. Despite many differences in the institutional setting, we find remarkable similarities when it comes to the performance issues facing boards. We are convinced that cross-national generalizations are possible. Boards around the world have the same broad goal—to govern their companies effectively—and they have the same constraints—limits of time and knowledge.

Our Perspective

THE IDEAS that shape this book come primarily from our experience. As directors and as consultants to boards, we have sat in dozens of boardrooms and have also discussed these issues with hundreds, if not thousands, of directors and senior executives in many countries who have deep knowledge of their boards in action. This book is a result of what we have learned from all of them, as well as from our own direct experience.

Our conclusions are supported by a brief questionnaire that around 130 CEOs of major companies from North America, Europe, and Asia Pacific responded to. The responses are highly consistent with our own experience. While this is not a large sample of opinion, it is a significant one, since these CEOs are all leaders of major global companies. And there is a remarkable consistency in the CEO responses from the different regions of the world—confirmation to us that boards everywhere are struggling with similar challenges.

It is to these struggles that we now turn.

two

Struggling Boards

"I constantly have to teach our directors. They really don't understand the business." — CEO

"I can't actually recall many instances when they [the board] changed anything." — CEO

"Our board satisfies all of the requirements of Cadbury, Greenbury, and Hampel, but our board meetings are a complete waste of time." — NON-EXECUTIVE DIRECTOR

A S WE SAID IN CHAPTER I, EVEN BOARDS THAT HAVE adopted the new ideas and best practices for board improvement are struggling to accomplish their mission. A gap seems to be growing between what they can accomplish and what is expected of them, and without explicit attention to board design, this gap will grow even more. To explain why we believe this is so, we first need to be more explicit about what constitutes best practice.

Today's Best Practices

A GRADUAL CONSENSUS about what constitutes best practice has emerged out of the ferment of the past decade. At its core is the basic proposition that boards must be *empowered* to govern well. The best way to achieve empowerment, the thinking goes, is to ensure that boards are controlled by directors who are *independent* of company management, and that directors' incentives are closely *aligned* to those of the shareholders. More broadly, the global corporate governance agenda is concerned with ensuring shareholder protection and high levels of financial disclosure: boards that are empowered, independent, and aligned are, in theory, the means to achieving these goals.

And in fact, the best practices that have been adopted by so many boards, especially in the United States, United Kingdom, and other English-speaking countries, are all intended in one way or another to enhance board power and foster "independent" thinking with share-holders' interests in mind. These practices include the following:

- Each board should have a majority of independent directors, and the definition of "independence" is becoming tighter. It not only excludes employees but also anyone who has had any recent relationship with the company as a supplier, customer, or professional adviser.

- There should be a leader for the board who is *not* the CEO. In many countries, this means that two different people will hold the positions of chairman and CEO. In other countries, such as the United States, where the common practice is for the chairman and CEO to be the same person, one of the independent directors will be designated the leader of the independent directors. In some boardrooms, this person is labeled "lead director" or "presiding director," and in others the leadership mantle is conferred on a committee chairman. Whatever the specific arrangement, there is an emerging view, even in the United States, that every board must have such a leader.

- Independent directors, rather than the CEO, should control the process whereby directors are selected for nomination and recommendation to the shareholders. Obviously, this will be based on consideration of the portfolio of skills and experience the board needs and should be done in consultation with the CEO, but it does mean that it is no longer acceptable for the CEO to be the major voice in deciding who sits in the boardroom.

- Each board should have three core committees—audit, compensation, and corporate governance (or nomination)—and their members should all be independent directors. In other words, the people who monitor management, decide how much they should be paid, and who should oversee the board itself should be independent. While this has been accepted best practice on many boards for several years, in the United States it is now mandated by the stock exchanges and, in the case of audit committees, by the Sarbanes-Oxley Act.

- The independent directors should meet periodically alone, without the CEO or other inside (executive) directors. This meeting will be led by the independent chairman, or by the lead director if the CEO is the chairman. Here, the independent directors will talk more freely and better understand their mutual ideas and concerns.

- Boards should be as small as feasible. A smaller group of directors will find it easier to interact and reach decisions subject to the need for enough directors to do the work of the board and its committees.

- Boards are expected to carry out certain activities, scheduled into the board's annual agenda, that provide another clear signal that the board is in charge of overseeing the CEO and the company:

  - Approval of their company's strategy, as developed by management, and an assessment of its effectiveness

  - Evaluation of the performance of the CEO and a determination of his compensation and tenure

- Oversight of the company's management development and succession planning, especially for the CEO and other senior management positions

- Evaluation of the board's own activities to ensure that the board is working in a manner consistent with these best practices and that board members, when being renominated, have been diligent and effective

- Directors should receive compensation that motivates them to focus on the interests of the shareholders; this most commonly is taken to mean maximizing shareholder value.

It is not possible to specify with any precision how many boards in any country have adopted these practices. However, it is clear that for most companies in most countries there is agreement among all interested parties that boards should have the power to oversee the company and management, and that most board members should be independent. It is also clear that, especially in the United States, more and more directors are compensated entirely or partially in stock and/or options.

Further, both anecdotal evidence and surveys by executive search firms indicate that more and more boards are adopting at least some of the other best practices, of course including those that are required or recommended by the stock exchanges or regulatory bodies. A growing number of companies have issued statements of corporate governance principles indicating that they observe these practices. What's more, the practices are included in corporate governance ranking schemes developed in the United States by institutional investors such as Cal-Pers, as well as Institutional Shareholders Services and more recently by Standard & Poor's (S&P), the credit rating agency.

Even boards that have adopted the entire current array of best practices, however, find the actual work of carrying out their responsibilities problematic. CEOs and directors alike consistently tell us this. It's a rare board that has been able to completely overcome the "disconnect" between best practice theory and implementation. Why? There are several reasons.

First, although most forward-thinking directors and CEOs now believe in the importance of board empowerment and independent action and aligning the directors' interests with those of shareholders, those beliefs don't translate into practice as intended. Some are even at odds with themselves and each other in ways that seriously undermine board effectiveness.

For example, it is true that boards need sufficient power to monitor their company's performance and even to replace the CEO if it comes to that. And it seems that in the United States, many boards have been gaining such power in recent years. Research indicates that given the same level of corporate performance, a CEO appointed between 1990 and 1996 was three times as likely to be removed by the board as one appointed prior to 1980.[1] (When John Akers was replaced by Lou Gerstner at IBM in 1993, it was headline news in all the media. Today, when a board ousts a CEO, the event is much less newsworthy. It has become almost routine practice!)

But increasing board power has in many instances made the relationship between CEOs and their boards more problematic. Clearly, although the board should have the ultimate authority to oversee the CEO's performance, there must be a reasonable balance so that the CEO retains the power to lead the management. In practice, though, the sharing of power makes the relationship between boards and their CEOs quite complicated. Each must avoid stepping on the toes of the other. And "power" is not a term that directors and CEOs are comfortable discussing with each other; it almost seems impolite to do so. (We'll discuss the intricacies of the director/CEO relationship in more detail in later chapters.)

Beliefs that have such fundamental tensions embedded in them can cause more damage than improvement in practice. What's worse, investors, lawyers, regulators, and others pressing for reform do not appear to recognize these tensions. Neither do the directors themselves. In our experience, these unrecognized conflicts can and do inhibit effective board performance. We shall name and elaborate on them in chapter 3.

Second, there is a significant gap between what boards are expected to accomplish and the time and knowledge available to directors to do their work. Put simply, the job is difficult if not impossible to carry out in the time most directors can devote to it. Because of that limited time and the rapidity with which business events occur, most directors find it difficult to keep up with their companies. The more complex the company, the more likely a director is to fall behind the curve.

Third, the director's task is becoming harder with each passing year. Businesses—regardless of the type of company—are increasingly complex, and investors and regulators are increasingly demanding. Consider, for example, the new requirements placed on audit committees by the Sarbanes-Oxley Act in the United States and the Smith Report on audit committees in the United Kingdom.[2] The raised bar is understandable—even justified. But most boards—even those that have been willing to embrace changes—are still bound too tightly to historical practices and traditions to handle their expanding responsibilities with ease. For example, too many companies still hold the same number of board meetings per year as they did a decade or more ago, and the meetings are conducted in pretty much the same manner, with the same type of agendas and boardroom discussions.

Fourth, these best practices do not always translate into action as well as they should because those responsible for their implementation do not have the time or perspective to think about how to make them work. They pay too little attention to the specifics of design.

Take, for example, the chairman and CEO of a major and very complex company who wanted to enable his board to approve and evaluate the company's strategy. As a first step he felt it was necessary for them to understand the major competitive and customer issues the company faced.

A two-day retreat was arranged for the board (no small undertaking in itself, given the directors' and management's busy schedules). The next step was to get the company's strategic planning staff to develop a series of presentations about the company's businesses around the globe. The plan was to have the board listen to twelve presentations by managers during the retreat. It was also decided to hold the meeting at a mountaintop resort (elevation, nine thousand feet) and to fly the directors in from all over the United States. Not surprisingly, the board members found it hard to keep focused and even to stay awake, especially after elaborate gourmet meals with wine.

While one might conclude that this was a deliberate effort by the CEO and his management team to subvert the idea of involving the board in strategic issues, we don't think so. It is just one of many examples we could cite where those responsible for board events (managers and directors) don't step back and think seriously about what they can accomplish in the time available. It's a simple example of poor design, but we believe that the failure of many boards to make the best practices work is the result of an accumulation of such minor design flaws.

Design, Not Attitude

HAVING EXPLAINED why best practices do not work as well as they might, we do need to reemphasize this point: It's also true that these practices do represent substantive progress in corporate governance. They have led to some important and positive changes in director attitudes. Most individuals serving on best practice boards understand that they're not seated at the table simply to do the CEO's bidding or enjoy a free lunch or be a rubber stamp. They recognize that they are serving to oversee management's efforts to create a prosperous company. This is a significant change from a decade ago. But this clarity of purpose isn't enough to overcome the limitations of the board as a group. Put another way, we believe that many of the problems facing boards have common sources, and it isn't the attitude or the level of intelligence of the directors or the intent of recent reforms. It's the basic design of the board in both small and large matters. Most boards are set up to fall short of expectations.

We've said that the problems begin with the limited time directors can devote to the task at hand, either learning about the company or in actual meetings with other directors, making decisions that directly affect strategy, management succession, and so forth. Let's look at these issues more closely, and explore how board design too often works against directors.

Since most directors today are independent non-executives, they are *very* part-time. In addition to their board seats, most have very demanding careers—they are CEOs or senior executives of other companies, or very busy professionals. Many serve on more than one board, although the growing demands on directors are leading to a decrease in the number of boards on which the typical director serves.

These part-time directors don't spend much time together. The vast majority of boards have regular meetings around every second month, and some only quarterly.[3] The meetings rarely last even a full day. While there is a growing trend toward holding an annual two- or three-day "strategy retreat," such as we have just described, that is the only evidence we've seen that boards are formally spending more time together in response to their more demanding jobs. In fact, according to one survey, the "average" directors in North America and Europe dedicate around one hundred hours or even less a year to their task (including time spent outside meetings on their own, gathering and reviewing information), with an average seven meetings a year.[4]

One U.S. director with whom we spoke appears to be fairly typical:

> The two large-company boards I am on meet eight times per year. One of these meetings is for a multiday offsite. So it's roughly ten days for board and committee meetings each year or about eighty hours plus preparation time and casual conversations with the CEO and other members of management. I think that the range is one hundred to one hundred twenty-five hours each year.

We'll tackle the *quality* of the time spent shortly, but for now, just consider the number of hours. An annual workload of one hundred to one hundred twenty-five hours translates into around two weeks of the life of a busy executive or professional. Think about what is expected to be accomplished in that two-week period—and remember that our non-executive directors are not only supposed to be very part-time, but because they are "independent," they start with limited knowledge of the company. The "median" North American director reported in this survey oversees a company with assets of $8 billion, 34,700 employees, production facilities in seven countries, and markets in ten countries. Over 40 percent of this company's sales are nondomestic.[5] Can directors of such a company, or even a smaller one, really be expected to do in around two weeks each year what those best practices suggest— review and approve business strategies and budgets, monitor performance, evaluate the CEO, oversee management succession planning, approve executive compensation, ensure that major risks are identified and managed, and that there is accurate and principled financial reporting, as well as general legal compliance? Remember, too, that all of this must be accomplished at board meetings where specific decisions like capital approvals, dividend actions, acquisitions, or divestitures are also considered, and where the board may also be asked to provide advice to management. It's no wonder that so many CEOs and directors themselves, as well as shareholders, are frustrated with the status quo.

Senior executives and CEOs tell us repeatedly that they question their outside directors' real understanding of their businesses. They are often frustrated by the apparent inability of these directors to absorb and remember what they have been told at previous meetings (small wonder, when you consider how crammed the agendas are for each meeting, and also the months that elapse between meetings). They wonder whether these directors know enough to understand and approve strategic moves and to judge performance.

Consider also the responses to several questions on our survey of CEOs—questions that dealt with how well non-executive directors carry out their tasks. Most of the CEOs agreed that in order to make major decisions about their company's future, board members need a clear understanding of what drives strategic success at the company, and of the major issues the company faces (see "What's Needed" in table 2-1). Yet only about half of the respondents said they believe their directors in fact have that understanding (see "What Happens" in table 2-1).

TABLE 2 - 1

Problems for Non-Executives—Knowledge About Their Business

	CEO RESPONSES: PERCENT AGREEING				
	North America	United Kingdom	Europe	Asia	Australia
What's Needed?					
• They must understand what drives success in the business (A-1)	98	94	97	100	100
• They must understand the major strategy issues in each of the major business units (A-3)	76	75	80	93	93
• They must be sufficiently informed to make decisions on major strategy moves (A-4)	96	94	94	71	100
What Happens?					
• They do understand the factors that drive performance in each of the main businesses (B-1)	46	38	51	40	53
• They often raise new issues in board discussion (B-4)	65	31	43	53	53

Note: The CEOs scored these propositions (indicated by letter and number, e.g., Proposition A-1) on a scale from 1 = Strongly Disagree to 5 = Strongly Agree.
For this analysis, scores of 4 or 5 were included in the "percent agreeing."

Source: BCG HBS Global Survey of 132 CEOs in 2001.

Similarly, CEOs and senior executives ask whether directors are familiar enough with internal candidates to make informed decisions about CEO succession, or whether they have the time to search for suitable external candidates. Again, the CEOs in our survey agree that what is needed is for directors to have knowledge about their company's talent—after all, it is the directors' task to oversee management succession—but at the same time, the CEOs believe directors don't spend sufficient time with these up-and-coming executives to gain this knowl-

TABLE 2 - 2

Problems for Non-Executives—Knowledge About Their Management

	CEO Responses: Percent Agreeing				
	North America	United Kingdom	Europe	Asia	Australia
What's Needed?					
• They must know the qualities of the executives who are candidates for the most senior positions in the company (A-5)	98	94	63	60	93
What Happens?					
• They spend enough time with management to be able to judge management succession issues (B-6)	63	25	17	14	53

Note: The CEOs scored these propositions (indicated by letter and number, e.g., Proposition A-5) on a scale from 1 = Strongly Disagree to 5 = Strongly Agree.
For this analysis, scores of 4 or 5 were included in the "percent agreeing."

Source: BCG HBS Global Survey of 132 CEOs in 2001.

edge (table 2-2). These business leaders do not challenge the board's responsibilities or question their seriousness of purpose in these areas, but they are uncomfortable with the directors' ability to carry them out.

The quality of contributions that directors make at board meetings is another concern that CEOs and even directors themselves have. What's needed, we are told (as the survey confirms), is for directors to do more than just ask good questions. They must be sufficiently informed to contest management's views. We have little doubt that directors want to be constructive and supportive, as the CEOs in the survey again confirm. The problem is that too often directors fail to focus on the critical issues, are insufficiently prepared, or cannot recall what happened at previous meetings (table 2-3). We have seen and heard this ourselves in too many board meetings, and the CEOs in our survey

TABLE 2 - 3

Problems for Non-Executives—Performance in Board Meetings

	CEO RESPONSES: PERCENT AGREEING				
	North America	United Kingdom	Europe	Asia	Australia
What's Needed?					
• They must do more than ask good questions; they must be sufficiently informed to contest managements' view (A-2)	76	81	83	100	80
What Happens?					
• They are well prepared for board meetings (B-2)	57	63	46	40	80
• They recall previous discussions (B-3)	52	56	63	67	40
• They often raise new issues (B-4)	65	31	43	53	27
• They focus on the important issues at board meetings (B-7)	63	69	77	67	60
• Their contribution is constructive and supportive of management (B-8)	89	94	83	73	73

Note: The CEOs scored these propositions (indicated by letter and number, e.g., Proposition A-2) on a scale from 1 = Strongly Disagree to 5 = Strongly Agree.
For this analysis, scores of 4 or 5 were included in the "percent agreeing."

Source: BCG HBS Global Survey of 132 CEOs in 2001.

apparently have had the same experience. The underlying difficulty is again the limits of time and knowledge. The problem is frequently compounded by inadequate attention to planning board agendas and meetings, and ineffective leadership in the meetings themselves.

For their part, the most frequent complaints we hear from independent directors are about the board agendas and how the time is spent in board meetings. Between "boilerplate" issues—the monthly results, dividend declarations, some committee reports, and even descriptions of legal issues facing the company—and CEO presentations on the state of the business, directors say that there's little time left for meaningful discussion, especially of major strategic matters. It's not that directors see the more "routine" activities as unimportant. They simply believe that they take up too much precious time. Such time would be better spent on the business and the challenges at hand, allowing directors to bring their own expertise to bear. One of the best ways for directors to learn and contribute, they tell us repeatedly, is by not just listening to presentations but by also engaging in discussion, especially with the CEO and also with other managers. But again, poorly planned meetings make this hard to achieve.

A major aspect of board design is the size of the board, and many directors also tell us that there are often too many people in the boardroom to allow real give-and-take—even if most of the people present are knowledgeable and ready to contribute. As one experienced U.S. director put it, "How can you have a meaningful discussion with thirty people in the boardroom?" In his case, there were eighteen directors around the board table and twelve managers seated along the walls of the room in case their "input" was necessary. This is a particularly large assembly, but the problem of too many participants in board meetings is very common. Most boards in English-speaking countries have around twelve members, and many have more. The number of people attending board meetings can easily swell to fifteen or even twenty when senior executives and outside experts such as lawyers and bankers are invited to attend.[6] It almost goes without saying that crowded boardrooms only exacerbate the time constraints we've already discussed. There are too many people who want to speak (either to offer comment, or to ask a question), while others feel inhibited about taking time from their peers.

Outside directors are also concerned about the flow of information they receive. Their biggest frustration is not that they get too little information, but that they get too much information that is neither well organized nor well summarized. Too much of this data, we are told, concerns past financial performance and forecasts; too little is about competitive performance, customer reactions, new product performance, the strengths and weaknesses of up-and-coming managers, employee morale, and the like. In some instances, as we have seen, executives feel that they have told the directors about matters that the directors have forgotten. Part of the problem is that the information has been buried in weighty board books, all of which cannot be absorbed and remembered by busy and part-time independent directors.

Despite the essentially positive adoption of best practices in so many boardrooms, it seems as though the picture is no rosier when looked at from the point of view of the owners, the stockholders. Many shareholders are concerned about whether boards are doing all they can to protect their investments. Large institutional shareholders are the most vocal on this point. Even before Enron and similar debacles, they complained that boards were too slow to act when companies encountered performance problems and the value of their stock plummeted. "Where was the board when things began to go bad?" is still the question on many shareholders' minds. Too many believe the answer is, "Like Nero, fiddling while Rome burned."

Institutional investors are increasingly scrutinizing board performance and driving for governance reform. In the United States, for example, the Teamsters' Union Pension Fund compiles a list of the United States' ten worst directors. While the criteria for the list might be vague, a clear point is made: "We are not happy with you guys, and we are vigilant in watching your performance." CalPers makes a similar point when it identifies companies that, in its view, are committing "corporate governance sins"—practices that either limit shareholder voice (like a poison pill) or indicate deviations from the new best practices, like too many inside directors, directors not owning enough stock, or outside directors serving on too many other boards.

The contemporary literature on boards urges adoption of the new best practices but is mostly silent on the practical difficulties of implementation that we have just described.[7] While many directors experience and feel in their "gut" the difficulty of their role, for the vast majority the epiphany only takes place when their company hits trouble. Suddenly they come face-to-face with a frightening reality: The company has gone downhill without their noticing it, and getting it back on track is going to require immense amounts of time—which they almost certainly don't have.

In summary, the concerns we hear from investors, CEOs, and directors convince us that, in spite of the progress made in many boardrooms during the last decade, the new practices are not enhancing board performance to the level that is needed. Boards are trying to raise their game, but they are impeded in this effort by working to a model that does not adequately recognize their central limitation—time and knowledge. Further, inadequate time and attention is being given to designing boards to successfully implement these new practices. Nowhere is the old saying "The devil is in the details" more true than in boardrooms.

An Even More Challenging Future

D IRECTORS' ATTITUDES have changed, and most are more seriously committed to meeting their responsibilities. The problem is that directors are essentially trying to make a refurbished 1955 Chevrolet keep up with the traffic on a twenty-first century superhighway. Directors will need to design their boards to implement current best practices and to move beyond them if boards are to succeed in the twenty-first century. And as we look to the future, the need to do this only becomes more acute.

This is because things are going to get even tougher for the boards of major companies. Business complexity is increasing—something most of us see daily in the impact of growth, globalization, and new technologies. New competitors are appearing, and industry value chains are being disrupted at a scale and speed never seen before. New financial products and techniques create greater risks. A fundamental change is taking place in the source of value in businesses from hard assets to human assets, and this also complicates the board's stewardship in ways that the governance discussion has yet to embrace.

These trends have been the subject of many books and articles, and we don't pretend to be experts on all of them, but we believe they make the tasks that boards face today and in the future very different from those facing boards of even a decade ago.[8] We will take increasing complexity of companies and the speed of change as givens, but there are three additional aspects of the emerging future that present significant challenges for boards:

- The effects of company globalization on board composition
- The impact of technology on one of the board's most important roles—approving business strategy
- The growing importance of intellectual capital as the driver of value creation

We'll look at each in turn.

Globalization

Global business is not a new phenomenon, but it is presenting new challenges for boards. Foreign operations are no longer seen as appendages to the domestic business. There is a greater commitment to building genuinely global firms, and boards are an inevitable part of this. Directors and CEOs (like those at Delphi) recognize that they need directors from regions of the world outside the home country, because they bring valuable understanding of these markets. One survey of directors around the world found that around 90 percent believed that companies with global operations should have directors from outside the company's home country.[9] But the practical problems are not insignificant.

If you add overseas directors, it likely means that the schedule of board meetings has to change. Traveling from Europe to the United States for a half-day meeting six or seven times a year, for example, is costly and a serious drain on directors' time. The logistics are even more difficult for companies in Asia, South America, and Australia because of the distances and the fact that board meetings in these regions are often held monthly.

Because of their location, so distant from other continents, and because their assets are increasingly offshore, Australian boards are being forced to address this problem ahead of those in other countries. The larger companies, such as the resources group BHP Billiton, now have a number of Northern Hemisphere-based directors. Given that a round-trip to or from Europe takes two to three days in travel time, each board meeting requires close to a week of a director's time. This board's response is to recognize the problem and to try to get the most out of each trip. The board meetings have been reduced from nine or ten to a more manageable seven each year, but each lasts more than a day, and some include site visits as well. The board meetings are also split between hemispheres to ensure that all directors see as much as possible of the company's operations, but no one set of directors bears the full travel burden.

Technology

Despite the bursting of the dot-com bubble, new technologies continue to have an enormous impact on companies' internal management, business-to-business transactions, and dealings with consumers. New technologies will also continue to spawn new products that will affect businesses profoundly. The results of all this will be immense and frequent changes to the ways that companies do business and inevitably to the knowledge required of directors.

Until recently, directors needed little or no real understanding of technological issues, because technology was simply a tool to implement a chosen strategy, much like a lathe or drill press. We don't need to understand how a car works in order to drive it, and the same logic was applied to computers when their main role was to make processes more efficient. Now, however, new technologies are themselves creating strategic choices for businesses worldwide. And the speed with which new technologies change today is stunning compared to even a decade ago. If directors don't have a reasonable grasp of the technology, they will be flying blind when it comes to the strategic issues facing their company.

Today, for example, it is a daunting task to be an outside director of a telecommunications company, a major bank, or a media conglomerate. Technology investments are of a scale and complexity scarcely imaginable a decade ago. It is true that many boards in these industries have overseen massive destruction of value and have been pilloried for doing so, but it is difficult to conceive of what non-executive directors spending only a hundred hours a year could have done to prevent it, especially without an understanding of the technology involved.

Marconi, a U.K. company, is a case in point. Formerly known as GEC—an icon in the United Kingdom—the company transformed itself over a few short years as management moved out of its traditional defense and electrical engineering businesses and invested heavily in high-tech telecommunications. The result, unfortunately, was a disaster for shareholders.[10] Clearly the task of overseeing a new and complex business strategy was daunting, especially in the limited time available. The challenging "design" question is to ask what the directors could have done to be more informed about what was happening.

Independent directors overseeing such complex businesses face a real problem. An experienced consultant working with the top management at another such company, this time in the United States, put it this way:

> It took us [the consultants] about four months of really hard work with the management team to get our minds around the issues. But we then had to "dumb" the material down for a one-hour presentation to the board. I felt sorry for them because, while they are smart guys, they didn't stand a chance.

For many boards, it isn't possible to have a real strategic discussion and provide guidance to management without a deeper understanding of technological issues than most of today's directors possess. That means that some directors are going to have to learn very quickly indeed, but it will take a serious investment of time to do so. Or we will have to rethink the skills and background of directors appointed to these positions.

Importance of the Human Assets

Consider the fastest growing companies around the world—biotech and pharmaceutical companies, media and entertainment, software developers, professional service firms, and manufacturers of new electronic products. The success of all of them depends on the talents of engineers, scientists, and other professionals.

This is a far cry from the days when the world's most successful companies tended to own the most costly physical assets—the turbines, the factories, the mines, and the wire networks that gave them competitive advantage and drove their profits. Value now is created more and more by intellectual rather than physical capital, a shift that has important implications for corporate governance in several ways.

First, the growing importance of human assets renders obsolete much of the long-running governance debate about whether boards are responsible to only shareholders, or to all the company's stakeholders. Second, the significance of human assets will require boards to rethink the issues on which they focus and the information they require.

Many advocates of better corporate governance around the world have taken the view that shareholder value is the prime goal of boards.[11] Dissenters from this view, often European, have lost ground if for no other reason than the overwhelming might of U.S. capital markets, which have been the loudest voice for such shareholder supremacy. It is ironic therefore that just as the shareholder point of view appears to have won the debate, it is becoming clear that a broader view also recognizing employees as one of the main drivers of value creation better reflects the reality of business in the twenty-first century. In more and more firms, what shareholders invest in physical assets is less important to success than the skills and capabilities of employees, as well as intangibles such as brands and customer loyalty.[12]

A cynic could argue that companies have always depended on their employees for success. This is true, but it's much more valid now than it was in the past. Many of today's successful companies in the industries cited have literally no means of creating value other than through the skills and talents of their people. And these are highly educated employees with a degree of independence and career mobility rarely seen before. A favorite phrase among top managers in the advertising agencies along Madison Avenue—companies that have always depended on intellectual capital—is, "Our assets go down in the elevator every night, and you aren't certain they'll come back up the next day." The boards of more and more public companies now share this concern. How do they ensure that management finds, retains, and motivates the talent they need?

While some managers may have worried about such matters in the past, boards, typically, have not. Directors have focused primarily, if not exclusively, on financial assets and the returns they generate. But we agree with management guru Peter Drucker that the focus must change.[13] Boards are going to have to find ways to oversee the state of their companies' human assets.

The question that boards will have to increasingly address is, "What is our role in companies where mobile intellectual capital clearly drives value?" What does it mean, for example, for the boards of companies such as Goldman Sachs, Microsoft, and WPP? What happens if a key group of investment bankers, creative directors, or software developers decide to quit and join competitors? How do directors think about such problems and balance the needs of shareholders and employees so the company can prosper? To answer these questions boards will need a value framework that calculates returns on employee contributions as well as on capital. They will need to understand clearly how to allocate excess returns between providers of capital and employees to preserve the company's wealth-creating capacity.[14]

Conceptually, boards have to think anew about who is "entitled to the rents." Historically, this was not in dispute. The shareholders rightly were entitled to the excess, since it was a return on their money. But today, if value disappears when key employees leave, there is a clear disconnect between the legal and economic ownership of the wealth a company creates. It means that it is hard for boards to think of businesses like these in any way other than as a *partnership* between employees and shareholders.

The growing importance of human assets challenges fundamental notions of who *really* owns the business. Legally, in most societies, the shareholders are still the owners, but in more and more industries, the employees must be considered to be owners as well, since their talent drives the results and the results disappear if they leave. This is a huge shift in thinking, to which boards must pay attention. Few boards yet have the inclination, let alone the time or the tools, to understand the ways in which value is created by employees, intellectual capital, and customer relationships, and to use this understanding to oversee their company's progress. Doing so is another very large challenge for the future.

Pressures for Change

NOT ONLY must boards contend with these challenges, they are also being asked to provide closer scrutiny and tighter oversight of their companies. The scandals in the United States and elsewhere in 2001–2003, as well as the prevalence of aggressive accounting and excessive CEO compensation in so many U.S. companies, made governance improvement in general and the reform of boards in particular a lead story in the media. Proposals for change have come from many directions and in many countries; from regulators, stock exchanges, from business leaders, and from newly established committees of inquiry.[15]

The best practice initiatives for board improvement are legitimate and well intended. There is, however, a basic problem with them, one we identified in the previous chapter. Many of these ideas for improvement focus only on those matters that can be observed from outside the boardroom. Focusing on what is visible may be the best way to put public pressure on boards to focus on "improvement," but it misses the essential fact that these visible factors have only a limited impact on board effectiveness. The real action is in the boardroom itself—how directors interact among themselves and with management and how they gain knowledge and reach decisions. Indeed, the challenge for all of us who are concerned about corporate governance is that most of the reforms that will truly make a difference inside boardrooms will only be visible to those who are seated around the boardroom table.

Some researchers have tried to find a connection between such external factors (as a surrogate for board effectiveness) and shareholder value, but we believe this is a very simplistic view of both what drives company value and the role that boards can effectively play.[16] The drivers of business profitability are many, and the relationship among them and their impact on shareholder value is complex. The competitive position of the company, the economics of its industry, the ability of management and employees, and the state of the economy are all major determinants of company performance and shareholder value.

Obviously, we don't disagree with the proposition that good governance contributes to corporate health. We do believe, however, that the way boards can contribute is *mostly* through their advice and oversight of management, and *occasionally* by being involved in major decisions about strategic direction and top leadership succession. And none of these activities can be observed unless one is a fly on the wall of the boardroom. Our own research supports our beliefs that external appearances of boards have no clear relationship to shareholder results (figure 2-1). For example, neither the proportion of outside directors nor the frequency of board meetings was found to be related to the total return to shareholders. What really counts is the dedication, energy, time commitment, and skills of the directors, the quality of their information, the leadership of board discussions, and the level of openness, transparency, and trust in the relationships among directors and with top managers.

The focus on externalities can actually have an adverse effect, because directors and members of management who work with them (corporate secretaries and general counsels) become concerned with these new requirements—because they feel they must respond to them. After all, the demands are coming from investors and other important parties. Yet time spent on these matters often does little to

FIGURE 2 - 1

Shareholder Returns Not Correlated with Governance Structures

S&P 500 FIVE-YEAR TOTAL SHAREHOLDER RETURN (TSR)* VERSUS BOARD STRUCTURES

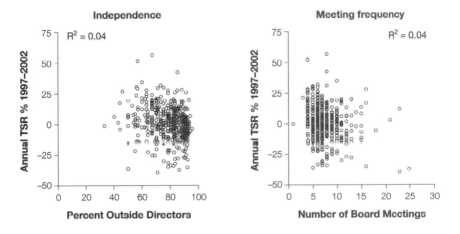

* Total Shareholder Return (TSR) captures the "total" return—both capital appreciation in the stock price and dividends received over a given period of time.

Source: BCG analysis of Datastream, Spencer Stuart 2002 Board Index data.

improve the board's effectiveness. Fancy statements about the company's corporate governance practices may look good in the annual report or proxy statement and make some shareholders feel good, but they don't in and of themselves make boards more effective. This problem was also recognized by the CEOs who responded to our survey. Over 85 percent of them—and the response was the same in North America, Europe, and Asia Pacific—saw the governance discussion too often focusing on whether the board of their company can "tick the right boxes" on some set of requirements rather than on the factors that truly determine a board's effectiveness (see appendix, Proposition E-8).

A final point: The answer to these problems doesn't lie simply in directors spending a little more time on the job. Yes, that will be a part of the answer, and already we see this happening. For example, the requirements in the Sarbanes-Oxley Act increased the workload for audit committees and the time directors must spend on audit committee work. Within a year of the time the law was signed by President Bush, we have heard about audit committees that have tripled the frequency of their meetings! But the quantity of time isn't the only issue, unless of course the role of independent directors is redefined to require literally months of work each year on the job. Rather, redesign of boards is needed to enable directors to perform better, within the limits of the time that they have available.

The "case study" that supports this view is found in Australia. Australian directors spend, on average, more than twice the amount of time on the job than do most of their overseas counterparts. A survey that we referred to earlier in this chapter found that they spend nearly 250 hours each year on their task, more than double the time spent by directors in North America and Europe.[17] Furthermore, Australian boards are nearly all led by independent chairmen and have a clear majority of outside directors, and so, at least on paper, these boards are empowered to do their job. The structures are correct, and the directors put in the time as well.

But it doesn't seem to make any great difference. Our experience with Australian boards is that they, too, are struggling. Directors, executives, and investors tell us that. In fact, the responses of Australian CEOs to our survey are similar to those given in other regions. Their directors struggle to understand the business, and the same frustrations exist.

To drive this point home even further, the same can be said of boards in the United Kingdom, where directors also spend more time than in North America and continental Europe (though less than in Australia). Again, the survey responses from CEOs in the United Kingdom suggest that the same problems exist there. In fact, a majority of CEOs in our survey (in all regions) are not confident that their independent directors understand their business, regardless of the amount of time they spend (figure 2-2).

In sum, in spite of the new best practices and the progress they represent, boards still struggle to do what is required of them, and will continue to struggle even more, as the demands on them are likely to

FIGURE 2 - 2

CEO's Aren't Confident That Independent Directors Understand the Business

PROPOSITION: INDEPENDENT DIRECTORS STRUGGLE TO UNDERSTAND
THE BUSINESS (% OF CEO RESPONSES)

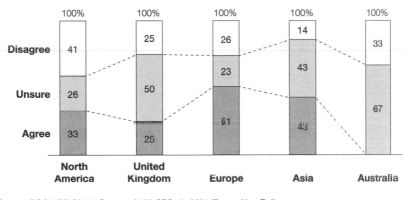

Source: BCG HBS Global Survey of 132 CEOs in 2001 (Proposition E-4).

increase. We've examined some of the immediate reasons best practices fall short of expectations. Now we'll take an even closer look at the practices—and at the assumptions that underlie them. Our belief is that the most promising solution to board problems is more careful design of each board. But not even a tailor-made design will suffice if it is based on flawed thinking about what's needed and why.

three

Best Practice
Contradictions

"The independent directors were smart enough, but the issues were so complex that they didn't stand a chance in the time available." —BOARD ADVISER

"If a board sets itself up as a policeman, they won't find the CEO very forthcoming with information." —CEO

"The recent scandals suggest that the idea of aligning directors with shareholder interest by having them own shares is not working." —FINANCIAL REPORTER

UNDERLYING THE BEST PRACTICES WE DESCRIBED in chapter 2 are five basic assumptions about the requirements for board effectiveness. These assumptions, which are generally shared by directors, investors, regulators, and other advocates for board improvement, are as follows:

1. Most of the directors should be independent—"the more, the better!"[1]

2. Directors should be financially aligned with shareholders through stock ownership and incentive compensation.

3. Directors should vigorously monitor management's activities and performance.

4. Directors should be "generalists"—all focused on their company as a whole (the only exception being the use of committees).

5. The primary task of a board is to create shareholder value.

These assumptions have had a great deal of impact on the composition of boards, on how directors approach their duties, and on how they are compensated. They've certainly had a positive impact overall on directors' attitudes. They have led them to be more active and empowered, and to take their jobs more seriously—to be more like the potentates that the lawmakers and shareholders expect them to be. And they're all reasonable assumptions, given the painful memories of past and recent board failures and excesses. The emphasis on independence has arisen because it's clearly undesirable for a board to be captive to management or for directors to have conflicting loyalties toward other organizations. Aligning a director's financial interests to those of shareholders seems a plausible way of making sure that directors focus on shareholder value. Because many companies have failed with their boards apparently sound asleep at the wheel, it's reasonable to emphasize the board's important monitoring role. Directors' desire to be generalists is easy to understand since they are each legally responsible for the success of their company. And the emphasis on shareholder value is consistent with the growing emphasis on the efficacy of market-driven economies. After all, efficient capital markets are key to economic success.

Yet as sound, sensible, and encouraging as they seem, these assumptions have serious flaws. And operating under them virtually guarantees unintended outcomes that inevitably cause serious problems for boards and diminish their effectiveness. What are the flaws? Think of them as *contradictions* that are embedded in the logic that underlies each assumption. Consider:

- Board independence comes at a cost. Directors who have no other relationship with the company are unlikely to know much about its business and will have a lot to learn. What's more, they will be very reliant on management in doing so.

- Aligning director interest with those of shareholders, by making them shareholders, can erode the directors' independence and even act as a catalyst for actions that are not in the interests of all the shareholders. Directors who own stock could think about what's in their personal interests as shareholders and not think broadly about *all* the shareholders.

- While good boards monitor and judge management's performance, they must also participate in key decisions and offer advice. Directors sit in judgment on management decisions to which they have contributed. This muddies accountabilities and makes the working relationship between board and management a difficult juggling act.

- "Generalist" directors, with only limited time to oversee complex companies, are likely to have a superficial understanding of their businesses. As the challenges described in chapter 2 grow, directors may find that the key to getting their jobs done is to divide their efforts and focus on specific issues.

- Shareholder value is of course an important goal, but in reality boards are responsible to a diverse set of shareholders who may have widely varying investment objectives and time horizons. Further, achieving long-term shareholder value involves meeting the expectations of others who contribute to company success— employees (as described in chapter 2), suppliers, customers, and so on. It would be easy if all parties could be satisfied in the same way, but invariably trade-offs among them are required.

Many of these contradictions are irresolvable—in essence we are talking about competing goods—and each board must make choices in finding the right balance between, say, independence on the board and knowledge of the business. So what's the best course of action? The important thing is to recognize the contradiction, discuss what it means for each board, and make the appropriate trade-offs in an informed and explicit way.

Taking a closer look at each of these contradictions will help clarify the issues boards need to consider.

Independence and Understanding

WE HAVE absolutely no quarrel with the idea of independent boards. Many of yesterday's boards were captive to management and essentially impotent. In other cases there were directors who were caught in conflicts between their loyalty to the company on whose board they served and other affiliations. The emphasis on independence is a way to mitigate such problems. Our question is, are we pushing the emphasis on independence too far?

Today, having as many truly independent directors as feasible has become a synonym for effective governance. This ignores the fact that there are other ways to ensure board independence. Further, this creates a difficulty that is rarely discussed. Having an overwhelming majority of independent directors means having a board that is likely to know little about the business or its industry. This lack of knowledge is particularly worrisome, since a good understanding of the business is something we've already flagged as critical to the effectiveness of a board.

The momentum toward independent directors is considerable. In the United States, around ten of the average twelve directors on an S&P 500 board are non-executives. Since the governance problems of 2001 and 2002, there has been even more pressure to ensure that these are truly independent directors.[2] Australian boards also have been mostly comprised of non-executive directors and therefore look much like their counterparts in the United States. In the United Kingdom, just over half of the directors on a typical board are executives of the company, but there is new pressure to have at least an equal number of independent directors.[3] In continental Europe, where practice has historically varied across nations, there is also widespread pressure to adopt the independent board model. In Germany, for example, where shareholder representatives—often senior executives of banks that have a financial relationship with the company—fill half the positions at the supervisory board table and employees fill the other half, applying the idea of independence is more complicated. Nevertheless, the recent German Corporate Governance Code devotes considerable space to avoiding "conflicts of interest."[4] The directors of leading companies in Japan and Korea are often executives, or executives from sister companies, but this arrangement also is coming under increasing pressure from global equity markets (and in Korea from government policy as well).

While the definition of "independence" can vary, it is clear at a minimum that independent directors cannot be employees of their company and should not have recent experience or relationships with companies that compete with it, or are its customers or suppliers. This rules out just about anybody who has firsthand knowledge of the company and its industry. Thus, most independent directors only gain their knowledge as a by-product of their board service—and given that the average director spends little more than two weeks a year on the task, it is a lengthy learning process even for experienced business leaders. For most part-time, independent directors who are busy with other activities, it is virtually impossible to develop much more than a rudimentary understanding of their companies' workings.

Furthermore, it isn't clear that a director can spend sufficient time in a business to adequately understand it without losing his independence in the process. If, for example, a director of a complicated company needs to spend several months each year on his duties, he should be compensated for this work. But today, a director "on the payroll" in this way could be viewed as having lost his independence.

Our conversations with directors confirm these problems. Many tell us that it takes them at least several years on a board to begin to understand the company in any significant way. Between board meetings they are generally busy with other activities. They have a demanding job and/or other directorships, and it's difficult for them to keep up with the rapid change that characterizes today's business world. Furthermore, because of those time pressures, they can't spend much time "on the ground" in the business—that is, learning about it through firsthand observation. Because they don't have that opportunity to observe the company and its management in action, they must be taught about it by others, and it's almost always the CEO or his direct subordinates who do the teaching. So if management's views are flawed, the board's will be, too.

The ironic truth is that the more independent directors there are on a board, the more reliant it is on management for information. When companies go into decline, their boards have generally been slow to respond to warning signs. A common excuse from board members is that they relied on information from management. Unfortunately, independence can make directors even more captive to management's view of the business—the diametric opposite of what independence is intended to achieve!

The proponents of independent board members, unfortunately, have not recognized this uncomfortable truth. Despite the differences across countries to which we referred, there is increasing pressure for boards to consist mostly of independent directors. But there is no discussion about whether this comes at any cost, and what to do about that cost.

We offer a different position. We emphatically agree that independence avoids conflicts of interest and dependence on the CEO, and provides an objective perspective. Board independence is a necessary prerequisite for one of a board's most fundamental responsibilities: unbiased oversight of management. However, we also believe directors need to understand the downside of independence, and find ways to overcome it. A more effective goal might be a board capable of taking strong independent action (and this means that a majority of directors should be truly independent) but also able to understand the company and its businesses (and this might mean having a few directors who do not pass the strictest "independence" test). If one or two of the nonexecutive directors have deeper knowledge of the company or its industry because of prior associations that prevent them from being classified as truly "independent," their inclusion on the board could be very much in the interest of good governance. Yes, protocols may be needed to deal with any conflict, but the board would be trying to achieve a better balance between independence and its understanding of the business.

It almost goes without saying that we also believe that boards must think creatively about how their independent directors can learn more about the business for which they are ultimately responsible—quickly and constantly and without almost completely relying on the CEO to do this. (In chapter 7 we provide ideas on how to do this, but we should emphasize now that there is no simple solution to the problem.)

We also believe that the attention to independence places too much emphasis on the independence of the *individuals* who make up the board. Certainly this is important, but there are also other design elements that can be used to ensure truly independent boards. For example, board independence can be promoted by ensuring leadership on the board by a director who is not a member of management and by making sure that independent directors meet regularly without management. We shall discuss these ideas in subsequent chapters.

Alignment and Independence

FINANCIAL ECONOMISTS introduced the idea of shareholder alignment into the corporate governance debate during the 1980s. The basic idea is straightforward.[5] The directors' job is to provide the best possible return to shareholders. Directors will do a better job if they think and act like shareholders. Therefore, directors should own stock, and the more the better.

According to this view, non-executive directors should be paid wholly or partially in stock and/or options, and should be required to own a certain amount of equity. They should have serious "skin in the game." The more stock that directors hold, and the more their compensation is at risk, the more aligned they will be with shareholders' interests.

Not surprisingly, this idea won enthusiastic support from many shareholder groups and some company directors.[6] It has been embraced widely in the United States, not only by boards but also by institutional shareholder groups and those who monitor board practices for them. Boards in the United States have totally rejected the traditional view that the truly independent director should be paid only with a cash retainer.

We have no problem with the basic principle of directors keeping their eyes on long-term shareholder interests. Our concern again is whether the argument has been taken too far. There was almost no criticism of alignment and remarkably little self-doubt among its proponents until the lessons from Enron and the other disasters of 2001–2002 confirmed what should have been obvious—that financial numbers can be seriously manipulated to paint an unrealistic picture of a company's financial standing. Management and boards, loaded up with stock and options, are subject to a potential conflict of interest. If accounting numbers were less subject to executive and director judgment and discretion, or even worse, to outright manipulation—the case for alignment would be more defensible. But unfortunately this is not the case. Attempts to achieve such alignment in some companies have thus led to directors' interests being aligned with management *rather than with the shareholders*. If management inflates earnings in pursuit of higher stock prices, our financially aligned directors may go along because they also stand to benefit.

The more shares a director owns, the more he has a personal interest to worry about—in effect, the more in danger he is of losing some aspects of his independence. And it's not difficult to imagine a situation where a director's personal financial interest in a certain outcome—an accounting treatment that affects the level of earnings, perhaps a decision around dividend policy or a takeover offer—is at variance with the interests of some or even most other shareholders. This is not to suggest that most directors are serving just to enrich themselves at shareholders' expense—in fact our own research and much anecdotal evidence indicate that financial gain is low on the list of reasons why most independent directors serve on boards—it is simply to point out the inherent contradiction in the ideals of independence and alignment.[7]

There is a further complication. The governance discussion about independence is mostly couched in terms of formal relationships. But the *psychology of independence* is different and arguably much more important. The longer a director serves on a board, the more emotionally committed she becomes to the company. Long service helps a director to understand the company better, but emotional attachment means she can't be truly independent. She identifies with the company, its management, and her fellow directors. She is certainly aligned with management, with the broader interests of the company, and its success, but may find it difficult to be truly independent in deciding what's in the shareholders' best interests.

There are difficult questions around this issue of alignment and independence, with no easy answers. Who, for example, is more likely to challenge a CEO effectively over his strategy or accounting practices—a relative stranger on the board, or a long-trusted colleague? The answer is, "It depends on the circumstances." We have seen both happen. But the assumption that underlies much of the governance debate seems to be that any director with a long-standing relationship with a CEO will be unable or unwilling to challenge him. We believe that this is a dubious assumption, but it underscores for us the complexity of the supposedly simple notion of "alignment" and how it might affect other desirable attributes like "independence."

The various scandals and accounting and compensation excesses that have come to light in the United States during 2001 and 2002 have reinforced the belief that independence is important. However, these same events have cast increasing doubts about the principle of alignment. If directors become too concerned about their own financial gains, they will be focused too much on the benefits to managers who received the same incentives, or to the interests of one set of shareholders at the expense of the broader group. Would a return to paying directors only in cash be a better guarantee of their true independence? It is worth thinking about!

Again, we have no easy remedy for these contradictions, but we do know that ignoring them won't make them go away. If directors can't at the same time be totally independent and absolutely aligned with their shareholders, how should they resolve this dilemma? This is a question that every board has to address. However, it should be clear that because the issues of motivation are complex, we cannot simplistically assume that loading up directors with stock and risk-based compensation causes them to do a better job. We think that the best way forward lies more in changing the design of the board and the way it works rather than assuming that throwing stock options at directors will motivate them to do their job more effectively. Part of each such design must be a careful consideration of what compensation arrangement will encourage directors to act independently and in the interests of all the shareholders and their company.

Advising, Deciding, and Monitoring

THE IDEA OF BOARDS being active monitors of company and management performance was first given prominence by William Allen, at the time the Chancellor of the Delaware Court of Chancery.[8] The speech was made at a time when many U.S. companies had been performing poorly and their boards had failed to act. So when an important judge from a significant court spoke, directors took heed, and the idea of monitoring as a key board responsibility caught on. More recent company failures and financial abuses in the United States and elsewhere have strengthened the belief that boards should take this responsibility very seriously. Boards today are ultimately responsible for management and company performance. If they don't like what they see, they are expected to make changes.

But directors also wear two hats besides that of monitor. The board also makes important decisions in its own right, such as approving plans or major investments, and in this sense the board is the company's ultimate decision maker. In addition, the board offers advice and counsel to the CEO. Establishing a relationship that allows all of this to happen simultaneously is very tricky indeed. It is truly difficult for a board to hire, evaluate, and possibly terminate a CEO while at the same time it is providing him with advice and expecting to have final say in many of his most important decisions.

The roots of this dilemma go way back. Old-style boards were full of the CEO's buddies. CEOs handpicked "their" directors, filling their boards with people they knew, liked, and trusted. They could choose agreeable friends or golfing partners, and many did. Over time, though, increasing numbers of CEOs also made it a point to look for directors who could also offer sound advice. The CEO's role is a lonely one, and many wanted directors who could talk about the business with them as peers. This shift in expectations on the part of the CEO was a boon for people who wanted to make a real contribution as directors; their roles became much more rewarding as they engaged more fully with the business challenges at hand. So the idea of directors being advisers caught on.

Over recent years, as boards have responded to rising expectations and their legal obligations, the director's advisory role has only continued to expand. CEOs today not only ask their directors for help at meetings, but also often contact individual directors between meetings to get their thinking on specific issues.

The problem is that boards are now also expected to "get tough" with management, to take charge. When companies fail, a key question is, "Where was the board?" Directors are expected to maintain very close scrutiny of management's activities—indeed, the monitoring hat is the most prominent feature of current best practices. But it is an inescapable fact that boards are also very much part of the management process—they don't simply delegate to management and periodically drop by to see if everything is in order. They are expected to make important decisions. They review and approve strategic plans and budgets; they approve management succession plans and executive compensation schemes. They approve risk limits and major capital commitments. They often approve senior executive appointments and major changes to the organization's design. In other words, they aren't just observers; they are active participants in the management process. And while individual boards may differ in the extent to which they delegate to management, most are more actively involved in key decisions than the boards of a decade ago. This raises two concerns.

The first concern is that there can be confusion about when directors are offering advice and when they are making a decision that management must accept. This may seem odd. Shouldn't experienced executives and directors be able to keep such matters straight? We agree they should, but the reality is that in the heat and haste of many board meetings, management sometimes can't tell which hat the board is wearing—and some directors often have the same problem, especially in retrospect.

The second concern is probably more serious and stems from the fact that directors' have asymmetric accountability. Boards participate in major decisions, but if things don't work out, they are rarely held accountable, because in addition to being decision makers, they are also the only real judges. Although one might argue shareholders should hold the board accountable for such failure, they really do not have the means to do so. Some would argue that this asymmetry is comparable to any other superior-subordinate relationship inside a company, but we believe it is unique. Inside organizations, bosses can fire their subordinates, but they are also held accountable for their subordinates' performance. CEOs have been penalized, even fired, for the failings of their management team. But boards tend not to fall on their swords when management fails, even where the board has discussed and approved the actions that caused the problem. Similarly, many CEOs have been fired for strategic failures, but we can't think of many boards that have resigned for the same reason. Even a catastrophic destruction of value doesn't seem sufficient to dislodge many boards. Even the Enron directors took their time in submitting their resignations!

This asymmetry in accountability can introduce great tension into what is already a complex relationship between the board and the CEO. The tension will often be reflected in management's reluctance to fully expose its thinking to the board. When this happens, the board's ability to perform effectively, of course, suffers. The U.K. CEO referred to at the beginning of this chapter pointed out to us that when boards become policemen, management becomes less willing to openly discuss its problems. It is a natural human reaction.

There is a big contradiction embedded in a role that combines adviser, participant, and judge, and this causes problems in many boardrooms. We agree with the increased emphasis on energetic monitoring that is a key feature of much of the advice being given to boards today. But it can easily conflict with the other hats that directors wear. As a result directors will find that none of the three hats are a comfortable fit. Boards will have to work hard to establish the working relationships with management that enable them to effectively wear all three hats at the same time. This requires considering how these three roles can best coexist, a subtlety that is rarely considered when best practice boards are being discussed. We shall examine in more detail the many hats directors must wear in chapter 4.

Generalists or Specialists

IMAGINE that ten capable people assemble to tackle a large and very difficult task. Let's also assume they each have only ten days each year to complete it—one hundred "person days" among them. Recognizing that time is their scarcest resource, the first thing they do is divide up the work, because they know it would be silly for everyone to try to do everything. The best way to succeed is to divide up the task, trust each other, and ensure that each member of the team carries his or her weight.

Boards, too, have a large and very difficult task, and not nearly enough time for each member to "do it all." However, they tend not to divide up the work. The only exception is the work of committees. Beyond that, everyone covers everything. They all deal with all aspects of the company, its future, and its performance. Directors are the archetypal generalists in a world that values and needs specialization.

One source of this contradiction is that, at least in the English-speaking countries, all the directors are legally jointly responsible for the "affairs of the corporation." This makes them reluctant to divvy up the job, even though any sensible assessment of the immensity of their task suggests that they should. But the legal issues aren't the only barriers. Some directors simply don't like the idea of a colleague knowing more about a subject than they do. They argue that boards shouldn't defer to individual directors on specific issues. Some also believe that by involving all the directors in every decision, the board will reap the benefits of their diverse knowledge and wisdom; often a valid argument. Others don't want the added personal responsibility of "owning" a particular area of the board's work. They'd rather share it. When all directors have the same task, they reason, it is harder to hold individuals accountable. Finally, some CEOs don't like their directors becoming more involved in specific topics because they fear that the board will stray too far into management's territory. Again, not an unreasonable concern, since we have seen instances when overenthusiastic directors stepped into management's prerogatives. For all of these reasons, whatever their merits, most directors want to continue being generalists.

As we have argued, directors in most companies are seriously challenged by the amount of work that they need to cover in the time they have available. With the growing complexity of companies and the resulting challenges boards face, the question of whether directors should remain generalists or focus on particular areas is likely to become a frontier issue. Continuing to have all directors focus on almost everything means that they are spread very thin, which is likely to produce superficial discussions and unwise decisions. Boards are engaged in knowledge work, and successful knowledge workers increasingly specialize or focus. Look at professions such as law, accounting, academic research, or journalism; all are much more specialized today than they were a few decades ago. Given the growing complexity of so many companies, there is considerable reason to believe that directors have the same need. In light of this, we believe that some greater specialization of effort among non-executive directors is both sensible and inevitable.

Directors' legal accountabilities are unlikely to change or diminish. In fact, they are growing. But assuming that each director has to oversee everything is not an effective response. Competence in complex matters is built on focus, and boards need to rethink the allocation of directors' tasks to allow more focused attention. New thinking about how to divide the workload and informed specialization is needed to ensure that time-constrained directors effectively handle the increasingly complex tasks associated with board membership. Such specialization will absolutely require that directors share their analyses and conclusions with their colleagues to ensure that all are comfortable with the work delegated to some. The challenge will be to do this in ways that do not encroach on management's responsibilities and which also keep all board members aware of major issues—and we will return to this issue in chapter 7.

Shareholders, Stakeholders, and the Corporation

IN THE ENGLISH-SPEAKING countries, beginning with the United States, as we have just discussed, there has been a growing argument that the only role of boards is to enhance shareholder value. Financial economists, shareholder activists, journalists, and many other observers have stressed this goal and the fact that boards are therefore accountable to shareholders.[9] This emphasis has gradually spread to continental Europe as well as parts of Asia and Latin America. The rhetoric in this direction has been so forceful that many, both inside and outside the business community, believe that it is an unarguable and unassailable fact.

Not true. Boards need to recognize that they have a choice to make in defining the goals of their activities, as well as the time horizons within which they intend to achieve these objectives. Beyond shareholders, even in the United States, boards do also accept responsibility to other stakeholders, such as customers, suppliers, employees, and the community, and they may decide that they are responsible for the health of the corporation itself. This broader approach is not necessarily inconsistent with their responsibility to shareholders. Taking a long-term perspective that focuses on the interests of these other constituents and overall corporate health is likely to support long-term shareholder value creation.

The debate about for what and to whom directors should be responsible has been going on for decades. For example, a 1989 study showed that U.S. directors were confused about their areas of responsibility.[10] Some of those interviewed believed their responsibility was only to shareholders. Others believed they had broader responsibilities to other stakeholders as well. A third group thought they were responsible for the well-being of their companies, and that in the long run this would take care of shareholders and others.

While the view that the board is responsible only to shareholders is still strongest in the United States, there are laws in thirty-one states that explicitly allow directors to consider the interests of stakeholders other than shareholders.[11] In Delaware, in which the majority of large U.S. companies are incorporated, the law specifies that directors are responsible for the welfare of shareholders and the corporation. In many European countries, boards are required to focus on the well-being of all stakeholders. In Germany, supervisory boards are required by law to ensure the long-term health of the A.G. (corporation).

Even those directors who believe their only responsibility is to look after shareholders' interests face a complex task in understanding what this means in practice. As we said above, it's unlikely that all shareholders will want the same economic outcomes in the same time frame. And who are the shareholders, anyway? The composition of the shareholder base in large public companies is dynamic and often unclear to board members. It is made up of a wide range of individuals as well as many different institutional investors with divergent goals.[12]

No matter how committed to advancing shareholders' interests a board may be, in the end it must exercise judgment about what the shareholders want in the knowledge that some shareholders may not applaud the outcomes.

If we look to the future, the idea that boards are responsible solely to shareholders becomes increasingly suspect. As we pointed out in chapter 2, while shareholders are legally the owners of a business, true economic and psychological ownership is increasingly in the hands of the company's valuable talent. Furthermore, executives running successful businesses (as well as their boards) know that shareholders will only be rewarded in the long term if customers, employees, and other important stakeholders are appropriately satisfied as well.

Boards have a real challenge in deciding to whom they are really responsible and where their commitments ultimately lie. Directors must think about and discuss among themselves the constituencies and the time horizons they have in mind as they think about the board's responsibilities. Many boards have skirted discussion of these complex issues. They seem too abstract, and reaching a consensus among board members about them can take more of that most precious commodity—time—than directors want to devote. Yet we believe it's important for boards to make these choices explicit, and to reach a consensus about their objectives for their company. When boards make a tacit assumption about their objectives but have no explicit discussion, they are hiding any disagreement among their members about what they are trying to achieve.

Resolving the Contradictions

IN THIS CHAPTER, we have described some of the difficulties that are inherent in the commonly accepted requirements for best practice boards. Director *independence* is widely demanded, but it will come at a cost that isn't being recognized. Financial *alignment* of directors has been advanced as an obviously good thing, but it can erode the board's independence. The board's *monitoring* role, so vigorously expected of boards today, can undermine the board's ability to carry out its other duties. Directors are still expected to be *generalists,* but this is likely to lead to a superficial engagement with the business. Boards are told to maximize shareholder value, but it isn't clear who the relevant shareholders are, nor is it clear that a wider *stakeholder* view isn't the more appropriate understanding of what drives success in many businesses.

In other words, making sure that boards work effectively is going to be a great deal more complicated than simply putting today's list of best practices in place. A lot of thinking is still required. So many of the emerging "rules" are necessarily confined to those matters that can be monitored and measured from the outside—such as the number of outsiders, whether they are legally independent (we can't monitor their psychological independence!), the leadership and committee structures and composition of the board, and the level of risk incorporated into non-executive director pay. But what happens on the inside of the boardroom is a much more challenging issue, and this is where attention must now be focused.

Something is going to have to give. Society must either reduce its expectations of boards, or boards must redesign their approach to governance. Such redesign appears to be the only viable option, since the need for more effective boards is so critically important. However, the process of redesign must start with each board having a clear understanding among its members about how they intend to approach each of the contradictions that we have described in this chapter. Not addressing all or any of them will leave directors confused about their purposes and goals and how best to achieve them. Sorting out these contradictions will not be easy, but if directors don't tackle the task, they will continue to waste time and energy. They will lack a consensus about how to deal with such fundamental issues as their goals, their roles, their rewards, and the attributes that their members must bring to the table.

Where to begin? The first topic boards must agree on is the role they should play. This is also the foundation on which sound board design must be built. It is the topic of chapter 4.

CHAPTER four

Different Roles
for Different Boards

"I want to add some value to this company. I don't want to manage it, but I want to be involved. I believe that I can and do contribute. And as a director, I don't want to be associated with a lemon." —INDEPENDENT DIRECTOR

"The reality is that you can do very little. So all a director should do is ask every six months or so whether there is reason to fire the CEO. If the answer is 'no,' then go back to reading The Wall Street Journal.*"*
—INDEPENDENT DIRECTOR

AFTER TALKING WITH HUNDREDS OF DIRECTORS over the past few years, we've come to realize that there is a widely held assumption that all boards do the same thing, and that each director, other than his or her committee responsibilities, has exactly the same job. Indeed, across industries and geographies, board responsibilities tend to be defined the same way. From Stockholm to San Francisco, from banking to beverages, statements of board responsibility list directors' duties as:

- Approving the company's strategy, plans, and budgets, and monitoring its performance against them

- Approving major capital expenditures and the disposal or acquisition of major businesses

- Approving capital structure, dividend policy, and the accuracy and transparency of financial statements

- Ensuring that major risks to the company are identified and managed

- Appointing and evaluating the CEO, and ensuring that succession is planned

- Approving senior executive compensation

- Ensuring compliance with legal and community requirements, and establishing ethical standards for the company

Directors, in boards of all shapes and sizes, for all types of companies, broadly assent to such a list of responsibilities. Whether a board has a unitary or a dual structure, and whether the chairman and CEO roles are combined or separated, its stated responsibilities are very similar to those of every other board. These responsibilities are consistent with the best practices described in chapter 2 and appear in many company and national statements of "board principles," as well as in recent World Bank and OECD corporate governance guidelines.[1]

The problem with such a uniform slate, however, is that it conceals a wealth of diversity and conflict at the individual level. Different boards face different circumstances, in terms of company complexity, company performance, the tenure and experience of their CEO, as well as their own capabilities. It makes no sense to assume that each board will undertake the same activities at the same "dosage" regardless of these differences, and indeed, despite the assumption that all boards do the same thing, our own observation confirms that individual boards do in fact undertake very different roles. (When we use the term "role" we mean simply the activities in which a board engages. As we will soon explain more fully, a board's role is the mix of monitoring, deciding, and advising involved in exercising its responsibilities.) But therein lies another wrinkle in the problem. We've also come to realize that the differences in the way individual boards approach their tasks are largely the result of tradition or habit, and that very few boards consider and choose the role that best suits their circumstances. Boards rarely discuss their roles explicitly. Nor do they change their role when circumstances change.

And that's what makes the great differences between the two quotations at the beginning of this chapter interesting. One statement was made by a director of an Australian company, the other by a director of a company based in the United States. Either statement could be considered acceptable in any of the countries where we've had experience with boards, because each board has a great deal of freedom in determining its role within the legal and societal context.[2] We don't like to think that any board is as useless as the one described in the second quotation. On the other hand, there is no guarantee that the more energetic director sits on a board whose activities best serve its own organization.

Put simply, while directors all over the world share similar views about what their duties should be, their roles and impact in practice may differ significantly. Further, there is no assurance that those duties add up to a role tailored correctly to the company a board serves. And since boards rarely talk about what their role should be, the cycle continues unbroken.

It is not surprising, therefore, that boards have no tools to help them think about their role. Yet we believe strongly that each board *must* define the value it will provide. It *must* explicitly choose the role it will play, and its choice must be informed by a good understanding of its company's specific situation and its own capabilities and talents. Defining its role is the first step in effective board design. It is as important as laying a foundation before a house is built. In this chapter, we hope to provide a framework through which boards can define their roles.

Realistic Expectations

W HERE TO BEGIN? Even if a board were to take the list of responsibilities we presented as a starting point, it would quickly be in trouble. Think about it. In practice, what can a board really achieve? How does an outside director spending a few weeks each year really approve and evaluate strategy for a company with dozens of global businesses? How well must a director know the executive group to understand whether a proper succession plan is in place? What does it mean to "monitor the performance" of a company? How deep into specific businesses can a board go? How does an outside director determine whether major risks are being well managed? And what does this list of responsibilities mean to directors of global giants like BP Amoco, Siemens, or General Electric (GE) who are overseeing businesses with revenues larger than the economies of many countries, as well as for directors of more modest-sized companies?

In chapter 2 we described how boards are struggling. This struggle isn't a function of boardroom laziness or incompetence (although we concede that some boards might be accused of both). In our experience, the central problem facing boards is that their job is huge, and directors typically have only two or three weeks each year to spend on it. And although common sense would suggest that directors should define their responsibilities as they pertain to their company, and then decide how much time they need, this isn't what happens. Tradition— of the company, of the country in which the board operates—generally determines the frequency and duration of board meetings, as well as the time outside meetings that directors are expected to spend. How all those duties are to be carried out (also determined largely by what's been done before) is then squeezed into the time available. The result is twofold: 1) As we've noted, boards around the globe may think they are doing the same things, but too few can be sure they're doing the *right* things in the right way for their company, and 2) the boards of huge global companies are likely to spend the same time as the boards of the local publicly listed widget manufacturers. That this situation exists is never discussed, nor are the problems it creates.

Spending much more time "on the job" is an unrealistic option for most board members; that reality only serves to underscore the need for the board's tasks and responsibilities (its role) to be defined. But it is critical, at the outset, to *pursue a definition that matches the resources available*. This means that every board must ask itself some important questions. What are we trying to achieve? What is realistic given our knowledge as well as the time we have available? What is our board's "value proposition" for the company and its shareholders? These questions will take most boards into new and unfamiliar territory.

Many Degrees of Freedom

THERE ARE really only two external constraints on the activities boards can and should undertake. The first is the legal framework within which they operate. In most countries, however, that framework is so broad that it provides little practical guidance. For example, in the United States (where the state of Delaware sets the standard), directors are told "the business and affairs of every corporation shall be managed by or under the direction of a board of directors."[3] The statute goes on to indicate that the board may delegate the management of the company to its officers. Beyond these broad statements, the legislation provides little guidance on the specific role a board should play. This is true of similar legislation in most countries. And even in a country like Germany, where the law is much more specific about board duties, the legal system still allows directors to make significant choices about the role they should (and wish to) perform.

The second external factor that might limit or direct a board's choice of role is the expectations of the company's shareholders. But here again, the influence is, in reality, minimal. For the board of a typical public company, shareholders' views do not determine with any precision the role it should undertake. (A board will pay attention to the views of the shareholders if one or more owns a significant stake in the company, which is more common in some European countries and the developing world than it is in the English-speaking countries.) This is not to suggest that directors can or should ignore shareholders' signals on governance issues even in a company with dispersed shareholdings; it is simply that public shareholders do not (and arguably cannot) provide boards with anything resembling specific guidance. As we have noted, they are a diverse group with different time horizons and objectives; their pressures for reforms are around specific matters that do not affect the board's role. In general, only when there is clear and unrelenting evidence that a company is in serious trouble do investors write to directors or request a meeting to ask for specific actions. And most wouldn't contact the board even then. Instead, they would follow the "Wall Street rule": sell when they are unhappy and move on to their next investment.

Boards are therefore largely free to define the role they wish to play. Spending some time considering the options, then, will help the board narrow in on the ideal set.

What Are a Board's Choices?

THE STARTING POINT in considering a board's options with regard to role is figuring out how *engaged* in the company the board needs and wants to be. And that means putting details aside for the moment and considering the broader picture. What kind of relationship does the board want to have with the company and its management?

In a study carried out over a decade ago, U.K. company secretaries who work closely with their boards reported that those boards were divided between those who saw themselves as "pilots" and those who saw themselves as "watchdogs."[4] This is interesting, if only as a discussion starter, because the labels imply very different intentions and levels of engagement.

Watchdog boards see their role as observing events; they only act if they sense that something is amiss. They believe that directors must be alert to what is happening with the company and its management, but their only real option if the company falters is to replace the CEO. If they are effective watchdogs, these directors smell the smoke before the fire is out of control. We see this set of activities as the least a board must do to meet its legal obligations in most jurisdictions.

A long time goes by between those moments when such a board adds real value. While the watchdog image is extreme, many serious observers recognize there are real limits to what boards can accomplish. For example, William Allen, former Chancellor of the Court of Chancery in Delaware, wrote that boards "are most likely to add serious value only in rare situations. On those occasions the problem will inevitably involve a CEO problem of some sort."[5] While boards do not like such a minimalist view of their role, most are quick to point out their limitations if their companies get into serious trouble. In his testimony during U.S. Senate hearings, Robert Jaedicke, chairman of the audit committee at the collapsed Enron, argued that the board's role in large, complex companies is heavily constrained:

> I see it as a cautionary reminder of the limits of a director's role. We served as directors of what was then the seventh-largest corporation in America. . . . The very magnitude of the job requires directors to confine their control to the broad policy decisions. . . .[6]

Jaedicke is essentially arguing that boards can *only* perform a watchdog role. In contrast, the *pilot* board has much higher aspirations. Its members believe that they should contribute to discussions and decisions about the company's direction. Like the first director quoted earlier, they believe they can actively add value to the company.

In the more extreme examples of the pilot board, the non-executive directors want to be very involved with management in making many key decisions and probing performance. This is very typical in smaller or start-up businesses, where management experience is lacking. Directors here might spend many days outside board meetings on the phone, engaged in meetings with management, and helping in what are essentially managerial tasks. This level of involvement is also commonly found among venture capital and private equity boards, where directors adopt a hands-on approach to overseeing their investments. They see themselves as part of the decision-making team, albeit on a part-time basis.

There are also examples of larger companies whose directors are far more involved than would normally be accepted. Delphi, described in chapter 1, is one example. Another was the Australian global property investor Lend Lease. Non-executives of this company were encouraged to be involved in some aspect of the company's operations for up to fifty days a year beyond the time devoted to their normal board duties and were paid for the extra time. Lend Lease produced stellar results for over two decades, making its novel approach to governance an interesting challenge to mainstream practice. However, the company's performance has recently stumbled, and the board has reverted to a more traditional form of involvement.

Most directors will resist both the extreme pilot and the extreme watchdog positions. They see the level of director involvement at Delphi and Lend Lease as inappropriate, a violation of that invisible line that separates management from board governance. They also reject the view that their capacity to add value is limited to waiting and watching for the occasional crisis. But, having dismissed the extreme ends of the spectrum, they struggle to articulate where between the two extremes they do wish to reside.

One reason for the difficulty is that although the watchdog and pilot labels are extreme ends of the spectrum, boards find the two are not necessarily mutually exclusive. A board cannot be a pilot without also being a watchdog. Furthermore, the terms do not help us to identify the specific activities that a board of either persuasion will undertake. For example, even the most deeply committed watchdog board will find it difficult simply to observe and react. It must be actively involved in certain decisions (e.g., selecting the CEO, determining his compensation, and approving new financing or a major acquisition). It must understand enough about the underlying causes of company performance to understand the extent to which the CEO should be held accountable for them. On the other hand, the board that wants a pilot role will still have to resolve questions about where to draw the line between its activities and those of management. It will also have to decide how it can hold management responsible for the company's performance if the board has been actively involved in major decisions.

Individual boards attempting to determine the right role, therefore, must get beyond these broad labels. The extent of their activism should be defined by what they want to accomplish. Their focus should be on the mix of activities in which the directors believe they should engage.

Think of it this way: All boards are always involved in some mix of three distinct activities:

- *Monitoring the company and management's performance.* This is clearly the minimal duty for every board. It cannot be shirked. Directors do this as they review financial results and listen to their CEO discuss the business at each meeting; as they conduct an annual performance review for their CEO; as the audit committee reviews the results of the company's annual audit with its external auditors; and in many other ways. Monitoring is a state of mind, a constant focus on how the company is doing. The question facing each board is how deeply and to what level of detail should and can this monitoring go? Should directors understand the performance of each business unit, or focus only on the company as a whole? What are the company's major risk exposures, and how does the board monitor these? What aspects of the CEO's performance should the board try to understand?

- *Making major decisions.* Every board has to make a few key decisions, but some boards make more than others. As well as deciding when and how to replace their CEO, and what compensation plan should be offered to senior executives, boards make decisions about major capital expenditures, and about acquisitions and divestitures, capital structure, and dividends. Some boards approve changes to organizational structure and senior executive appointments. Some approve risk limits. Some delegate only a little; others delegate a great deal.

- *Offering advice and counsel to management, especially the CEO.* In some instances, the CEO explicitly asks the board for advice. In others, the directors offer advice as an alternative to either approving or turning down a management proposal. In both situations, the directors are offering management the benefit of their experience and wisdom. Whether this counsel is accepted or ignored is likely to depend on how emphatic the directors are in their views and how confident the CEO feels about her own and her management team's judgments. The important point, however, is that advice is different from a board decision. In the latter case the board has the final word, but in the former the CEO and her management team have a choice. They can decide to accept the board's advice, ignore it, or continue a dialogue until agreement is reached.

In our experience the particular mix of these three types of activities really defines a board's role. The more decisions a board insists on making or approving, the closer it is to the pilot end of the spectrum. It may not be stepping on management's toes, but it is certainly becoming more of an active partner in shaping the company's destiny. On the other hand, a board that limits itself to monitoring company performance, offers little advice, and is involved in few decisions is clearly in more of a watchdog mode. It's useful at the outset for directors to have a "gut feeling" about whether the board should be more of a watchdog or a pilot, but ultimately, an objective consideration of the mix of activities, based on what the company needs, must be made.

Thinking About the Board's Role

TWO FACTORS should drive the way a board thinks about the mix of monitoring, deciding, and advising that define its role. The first is the circumstances of the business. If the business is in trouble or the industry is going through momentous change, the board may need to be more engaged than it otherwise would. The second factor concerns the directors' capabilities and preferences. Boards must ask themselves what skills they can contribute and how much time they can devote. And they must decide how comfortable the directors are about delegation to management (e.g., how confident are they in their CEO's ability and judgment?) because this too will have an influence on the role the board adopts.

Company Circumstances

Is the company in trouble or going through a period of great change? Is the CEO well established and performing well? What kind of relationship does the board want to develop with him? And what might the owners' wishes be?

Business Performance

The obvious starting point to answer such questions is the company's financial condition. If it has been performing well year after year and has a strong balance sheet, the directors may conclude that they should sit back and monitor events. "If it ain't broke, don't fix it." This is a rational position under such conditions, but there is risk in adopting it. Boards of companies that are performing well can become complacent, but unfortunately nothing is forever in the business world. The CEO who has been central to the company's success might become ill or decide to retire. If he and the board haven't worked together on succession, the company could falter. Or a new competitor with a superior business model could emerge. If the company's financial performance drops as a result, the board and management could be caught flatfooted. Even the most detached of boards must be prepared for events like these.

Complexity of the Business

We focus on complexity rather than size because extra zeros before the decimal point on the revenue line don't necessarily make a company harder to understand. A large company in a single business, even if it operates around the world, is easier for a board to understand than a company that operates many different businesses. Directors of a global fast-food company, such as McDonald's, or a major airline, such as British Airways, will find it easier to understand their company than do the directors of a smaller company with multiple lines of business, such as the Brunswick Corporation, which manufactures boats, marine engines, and fitness equipment, as well as operating bowling centers and manufacturing bowling equipment. Directors in the former type of company need to understand the key strategic factors in a single business, while those overseeing a more diversified company have the challenge of comprehending the factors that contribute to success in multiple businesses. Directors need to consider the extent to which they should understand individual businesses, as well as how much they trust management's capacity to oversee those businesses if the board focuses only on the larger corporate picture.

Industry Turbulence

Industry turbulence is closely related to company complexity. Directors of a company in an industry characterized by rapid technological change and the frequent arrival of new competitors face greater challenges than directors of companies in more stable environments. Would it be easier to be a director of a company like Coca-Cola or PepsiCo, in an industry where the major players are identified and the competitive rules well established, or of a high-flying biotech firm dealing with a constant flow of new products and new competitors? Even in well-established industries, the dynamics of decline and consolidation can present boards with a significant challenge. Consider, for example, the task facing the directors of European telecommunications companies in recent years. Rapid changes in industries or markets call for more engaged boards. How should a board approve strategy, monitor performance, and oversee major risks in these circumstances?

Relationship with the CEO

Whatever role the board chooses, it can only accomplish this by working effectively with the company's CEO. Directors certainly understand this, and so do CEOs. However, boards are rarely explicit about figuring out the best way to do this. More often than not, the relationship simply evolves. But if the board's role and its desired relationship with the CEO are unclear, the result can be a breakdown in trust.

We have seen, for example, a newly minted CEO and chairman in a U.S. company, one with very limited board experience, decide "to straighten my board out." Believing the board was inefficient and wasting time, he tried to change committee chairs and members, the nature of board agendas, and the type and pace of board discussions without consulting the board. The directors were appalled. They had selected him as CEO because of his success as an operating executive and believed he had great potential as the company's leader, but they also quickly concluded that he needed more experience in working with them. As far as they were concerned, his autocratic attempts to improve the board proved their point, and his efforts met with disapproval and resistance.

In this instance, the arrival of a new leader did not prompt the board members (including the CEO) to decide explicitly the way they should work together. In such a situation, many directors are inclined to think, "We've got a new unproven guy, we better tighten up the reins a bit," but they rarely take time to reassess the board's role in light of the changed leadership. We believe the directors and the new CEO should talk frankly and explicitly about how they are going to work together.

It is also true that the relationship between the board and the CEO can change over time, which again should prompt a reassessment of the board's role. The board may want to be less actively engaged as the CEO builds a track record of success and the board's confidence in her leadership increases, or the opposite may hold. Either way, we firmly believe that any change to the board's role or its relationship with the CEO should be explicitly discussed, among the directors themselves and also with the CEO.

Finally, many CEOs are understandably ambivalent about pilot-type boards. Left to their own devices, they would prefer a nonbarking watchdog that allowed them to run the company in their own way.

However, CEOs must accept the need for their boards to define their own roles even though, with corporate governance under the spotlight as it is today, this can result in a board role that the CEO finds problematic. The best way to deal with this is to ensure that the directors and the CEO explicitly discuss the matter, so that everyone at least has a shared understanding. The role the board adopts might not be exactly what the CEO prefers, but at least he will have a clear idea of how the board will operate and what he will need to do to build a productive working relationship.

Shareholder Requirements

Another issue to consider is the ownership of the company and the shareholders' goals. The board of a start-up company, for example, owned by its founding managers and the investing venture capitalists, usually has a very clear sense of what these shareholders want—to move the company through to a successful IPO. This aspect of the directors' role is clear. They need to govern to achieve this end.

However, the more common situation facing the directors of a large, established public company is that they have an incomplete understanding of what their diverse shareholder base wants. It is easy to get a list of a company's fifty largest shareholders, but that is not the same as understanding whether they have common investment goals. If directors cannot figure out their shareholders' expectations, we believe they should at least be clear about their own goal as a board. Is it to create shareholder wealth in the short term or, on behalf of shareholders and other stakeholders, to ensure the longer-term success of the company? Directors cannot decide on the appropriate role to adopt if there is no clear consensus among them on the board's overall objectives. What results do they want to achieve, and in what time frame? We believe this is essential because of the pressures so many boards and managements are under from analysts and money managers, who demand quarter-to-quarter earnings growth. If directors are not clear about their goals for the company, they are likely to find themselves succumbing to these pressures.

Board Style and Capability

In determining their role, boards also need to understand what they bring to the equation. Whatever the role they'd *prefer* to perform, do they have the resources and capabilities to carry it out? And what is the right level of delegation to management, given the directors' capabilities and style preferences?

Board Resources and Capabilities

As we have seen, boards have two fundamental resources with which to work. One is the time that non-executive directors can and will commit to board work. The other is the directors' combined experience and knowledge, and especially what they know about their company. These two are obviously related—the more time directors spend considering and discussing their company, the deeper their knowledge about it should be.

As we have pointed out, we are concerned about directors being pressed to take on more and more activities, without an increase in the time they devote to board work. Exactly how much time directors of public companies spend on board work is not entirely clear, but as we reported in chapter 2, it is unlikely in most countries to be much more than around one hundred hours each year.[7] We see time as an overarching constraint on the role any board adopts, but we also believe this can be changed if the directors are committed to doing so, and if they are appropriately rewarded.

In the aftermath of Enron, along with the heightened requirements imposed by the Sarbanes-Oxley Act and new listing requirements by the stock exchanges in the United States, we have an excellent example of the pressures boards can face in getting their members to spend more time on board work. In the short term, U.S. directors, especially those on audit committees, seem willing to step up to the challenge. It remains to be seen, however, whether this commitment will hold in the longer term, given directors' busy lives and the reward structure that now exists.

Aside from time, boards must also have the right information and knowledge to perform their chosen role. This brings us back to the dilemma of independence and understanding we described in chapter 3. Stated simply, independent directors usually start with a knowledge disadvantage. The problem is ameliorated to some extent with tenure on the board, because directors learn as they serve. But even after long service, and especially in complex and dynamic industries, directors often find that the limits of their knowledge and understanding place real constraints on the role they can play.

Since most boards struggle to build the knowledge required to carry out their responsibilities, directors need to decide when they should become more deeply engaged. Vinny Learson, former CEO of IBM, used to talk about "bet the company decisions"—ones that, if they turned out to be wrong, could literally sink the company.[8] For most companies, such decisions are few and far between, and these are the points where, at a minimum, the board becomes deeply involved. In thinking about their role, directors need to understand which types of decisions are central to the company's future. Even a board that is gravitating toward the watchdog end of the spectrum will want the final voice in decisions of this magnitude.

As directors consider the resources of time and knowledge available to them in relation to the role they feel they should undertake, they must be objective and realistic. It is easy for enthusiastic directors to lose sight of the real constraints they face. A board that attempts to adopt a role for which it has neither the time nor the knowledge is likely to be as unsuccessful as one that hasn't considered its role at all.

Delegation Preference

The level of involvement that a board chooses will also reflect the directors' personal leadership styles. Some directors strongly believe that it's management's job to run the business and the board's job to decide whether the outcomes are satisfactory. A board dominated by directors with this mind-set may engage in the activities common to all boards, but will do so in a very hands-off manner. It will be involved in fewer decisions. It will tend not to advise the CEO unless she specifically requests it. Its members will likely have little involvement with the company outside board meetings.

Other directors will prefer to be more involved. They will delegate less to management and want to share responsibility for leading the company and approving key decisions. Directors with this mind-set and leadership style will find it hard, perhaps impossible, to adapt to a board role that is much more about observing and judging than acting and contributing. They will prefer to be toward the pilot end of the spectrum.

There is no "right" leadership style for boards any more than there is for any other leadership job, but in determining the role a board will play, it is important to understand where directors stand on this matter, and how that might affect the activities the board wants to undertake. If the directors have not agreed among themselves and with the CEO on the role they feel comfortable taking, confusion and dissatisfaction can easily be the result.

A Framework for Thinking About Role

BECAUSE the board's job is large and directors' time is limited, every board must decide how deeply engaged it should be in company decisions, how much it wants to be involved in providing advice, and what aspects of performance it chooses to monitor. It's clear that there is no simple formula for determining this mix, and therefore what role a board should adopt.

Further, the same conditions can pull a board in opposite directions. For example, on the one hand, rapid change and complexity might suggest that the board play an activist role. On the other, these conditions make it more difficult for directors with limited time to keep abreast of events and contribute to decisions. They might argue that a little knowledge is particularly dangerous in a demanding and fast-moving situation. How can boards work through such issues?

Directors can ask themselves whether they want to be watchdogs or pilots, but this is only a starting point, as we've said. To determine how engaged directors should be and what mix of advising, decision making, and monitoring they should adopt, it is obviously necessary for them to consider their company's circumstances and their own capabilities. Each board needs to ask itself these questions:

- *To what extent do directors want to be informed advisers to the CEO?* How much will they need to understand to be able to provide good advice rather than just ask good questions? When management explains its strategy or presents an investment proposal, should the board know enough to really challenge management's views? How much due diligence will be needed? Or will it suffice for the board to simply provide comments based on their prior experience?

- *What will be involved in monitoring the performance of the CEO and the company?* Can the board rely on aggregate outcomes (e.g., company profitability) or does it want to understand what is happening to the main drivers of performance in different businesses? If directors want the latter, how do they learn about it, given the size and complexity of the company? How deep in the company should the board delve for information? How much time will it have to spend, and what activities will it need to undertake to get the needed information?

- *What variables does the board want to monitor most closely (e.g., financial performance, competitive positions, risk exposures, management succession and development, employee morale, customer satisfaction)?* How frequently and in what detail does the board want information on these matters? Will it rely on management's word or will it conduct an independent exploration? What *exactly* does the board need to do and know if it is to have any chance of smelling the smoke before the fire is out of control?

- *How extensively does the board want to be involved in setting and evaluating strategy?* Should it confine its interest to issues at the corporate level, or does it want to be familiar with the main strategic issues in the company's larger businesses or even all its businesses? And is the board happy to be informed about management's intentions after the strategy has been developed, or does it want to play a part in that development?

- *What decisions and approvals are the board's domain rather than management's?* Do these include, for example, aspects of strategy, capital and operating budgets, risk limits, acquisitions, divestitures, senior executive appointments, and top-level organization design? If the board is going to approve specific capital expenditures, what level will require its approval? What reasons does the board have for making these choices?

Discussions about these questions will bring a board as well as management to a better understanding of the board's role. When directors differ on some of the details, the differences will be brought into the open, where they can be understood and resolved.

It may also be desirable to talk about specific examples from the board's past experience, because many of us put different meanings to the same words. For example, to "monitor" or "review" may mean different things to different directors. Discussing recent specific cases will uncover whether the directors among themselves and with management really do have a shared understanding. If an acquisition turned out poorly, what might the board have done differently? Was the board's level of involvement in the recent strategy process about right? Should the board have been consulted before the CEO changed the top-level organization structure?

Focusing on such questions and discussing prior experience will take the board into quite some detail. Once there is a consensus around the answers to these questions, it is possible to step back and define at a broader level the role the board intends to play—how engaged it will

FIGURE 4 - 1

Framework for Defining Board Involvement
(DAYS EACH YEAR PER DIRECTOR)

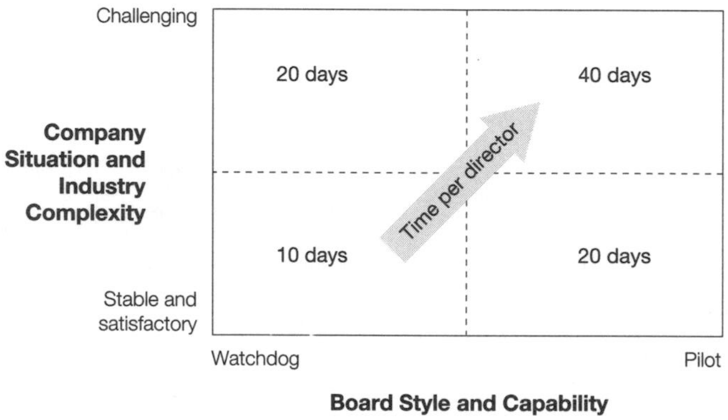

be in monitoring, advising, and decision making, and what the mix of these should be.

A concrete way to test whether the role the board is defining for itself is really doable is to try to estimate how much time directors are going to have to commit. We have made an estimate of this, given the role a board chooses (figure 4-1). Our estimates provide a starting point for another discussion that simply doesn't take place on most boards: How much time do we need to spend if we are going to do this job properly? Notice that what we see as a minimum commitment—ten days or around eighty hours per year—is already not too far from the North American average of one hundred hours a year. This leads us to the inevitable conclusion that many directors will have to spend more time in the future.

If a board decides to adopt a watchdog role only, a time commitment ranging from ten to twenty days per year might suffice, depending on the complexity of the business. This board's primary focus will be on ensuring sound monitoring processes. Our sense is that the monitoring role has become ritual in many companies, and a board that is serious even about this fairly minimalist stance will need to step up its probing activity. This is likely to involve increasing the attention given to internal and external audits, expanding risk management checks, and the like. It might also include more attention to post-investment audits: Did we achieve what we expected to achieve?

If a board in a complex company undergoing significant change wants to move toward the pilot end of the spectrum, to be seriously involved in major strategy discussions and decisions about major business issues, directors may need to seriously expand the time they spend. Our guess is this could require forty days a year, at least until their company's problems are ameliorated or the environment becomes more stable. But even at this level of commitment, the directors of complex companies must be selective about where and how they engage. The board is likely to focus more on corporate rather than business unit strategy, unless a couple of businesses dominate the portfolio. Board discussions will concentrate on the shape of the portfolio—which businesses are candidates for disposal, where are the growth opportunities, and what are the main value-creating opportunities and difficulties? As we mentioned earlier, even very engaged boards may have to limit deep engagement to "bet the company" issues. But we can't imagine, for example, how a non-executive director on the board of a major telecommunication company could have done a passable job over the last few years without devoting extraordinary amounts of time to board work. These companies placed some huge bets in an environment of extraordinarily rapid technological change. Looking back, we can see that some of their investments in new technologies have led to enormous destruction of shareholder value. Could these boards possibly have had the time and knowledge needed to approve those investments?

Whatever the level of board engagement, however, delegation to management will always be substantial, because whatever role the board adopts, non-executive directors cannot be management. Directors, even on the most active boards, can only be involved in significant decisions and oversight of the company's performance. However, boards can and should make a conscious decision on how detailed their oversight is to be and how much time the directors should spend "kicking the tires" inside and outside the company.

Different Answers for Different Boards

EVERY BOARD will have its own answer on its role, and we believe the future will see much more differentiation around this issue. From company to company, across geographies, boards will be less alike and certainly less captive to long-established traditions. One approach will not be forced on all boards. The best answers will reflect the demands of the situation. Further, boards must rethink their roles as circumstances change. For example, boards that elect to be heavily involved in decision making with a new and untested CEO may reduce this involvement as the CEO gains experience and success and the board gains confidence in him.

The idea of each board defining its own role is not addressed in much of the literature on boards. Further, the dividing line between the board's role and that of management is assumed to be fixed. Many writers on governance assert that all directors have the same job and that their work is fundamentally different from that of an executive.[9] *Governing* and *managing* are held to be quite distinct from one another. If we accept this, the task of deciding how involved a board should be becomes constrained by definition—directors are barred from any task that management undertakes.

The distinction is unhelpful because it diverts us from dealing with the full complexity of defining the board's role. Boards on some occasions may decide to involve themselves in tasks that are usually considered to be management's. Further, the distinction can also cause confusion because the role of even the most minimalist board is a part of the company's management process. The distinction between governance and management is not cut-and-dried. When directors approve investments and risk limits, when they sign off on the strategy and budget, when they monitor performance, and when they offer advice, they are doing exactly what the senior management team does, but they are usually focused only on the most significant issues faced by the company as a whole.

This way of looking at things may make some managers and directors very uncomfortable, because it blurs the supposedly sharp line between board and management responsibilities. But let us illustrate our point with an example: two 1990s competitors in the global pacemaker business. Medtronic, U.S.-based and the world's number one, was largely a single business enterprise, whereas the world's number three, Telectronics, was owned by Pacific Dunlop, an Australian-based sprawling conglomerate. The oversight activities undertaken by the Medtronic board in relation to its pacemaker business were very different from those undertaken by the Pacific Dunlop board in relation to Telectronics.[10] The Telectronics business was one of many in the Pacific Dunlop portfolio, and the board could only spend a small fraction of its time on it, whereas Medtronic's board deeply understood and more closely followed its pacemaker business. But the responsibilities of each board were the same. The difference was that the Pacific Dunlop board delegated many of the activities undertaken by the Medtronic board to executives in its corporate center. In the late 1990s, as Medtronic acquired other medical device businesses, the board's attention was focused on all of these businesses and, as a consequence, less intensely on the pacemaker business.

In practice, therefore, we cannot define a board's role in a way that draws a clear and straight line between it and management. Boards will choose different levels of involvement and will delegate more or less to management. In some instances, their activities will be very much a part of the management process.

We also must remember the growing gap between society's expectations and what a board can truly achieve. The sheer complexity of today's businesses and the practical limits we have discussed on directors' time mean that boards simply can't achieve everything that is expected of them, even if they do devote more time to their board duties. Legally, directors are responsible for the company even if they delegate almost completely to management. However, the scope of this responsibility is hard to reconcile with the limits of time and knowledge that independent directors must live with. Boards that clearly understand their roles will use their limited resources better because their efforts will be much more focused.

The Board of the Future

IF EACH BOARD defines its role explicitly, there will be a substantial change in the way boards function. Boards will become more differentiated in their composition and activities.

While there may be increased time commitments for many directors, boards will focus clearly on their major tasks, rather than trying to do everything.

There is support for this from the CEOs in our survey. Cynics might expect CEOs to take every opportunity to diminish their boards' involvement in their businesses. But this is not what they are saying. The survey responses, taken before the Enron and later debacles, indicate that these CEOs want directors to increase the time they devote to board business. They also reject the notion that the board's scope ought to be reduced so that boards can be more effective (table 4-1).

We have talked about the mismatch between what boards are being asked to do and the resources they have available. However, we believe the broad job description for directors is unlikely to change in the near term. It is broad because directors sit at the apex of complex businesses and are legally responsible for their performance. We also believe that in spite of the fact that CEOs, investors, and regulators ask directors to spend more time on their duties, this is unlikely to happen to any great extent in the foreseeable future. But by carefully defining their board's role, directors *can* more effectively use their limited time.

Boards do face real choices in their role. We have no preference in terms of the range from watchdog to pilot. What is critically important is for each board to reach a consensus about the role it intends to play and then to do it. This then will become the foundation on which the

TABLE 4 - 1

More Time Required and No Narrowing of Scope for Independent Directors

	CEO RESPONSES: PERCENT AGREEING				
	North America	United Kingdom	Europe	Asia	Australia
• They must spend more time on the job (C-1)	54	69	66	73	53
• The scope of the board's role and accountability will have to be narrowed in order for them to be more effective (C-7)	11	12	20	20	20

Note: The CEOs scored these propositions (indicated by letter and number, e.g., Proposition C-1) on a scale from 1 = Strongly Disagree to 5 = Strongly Agree.
For this analysis, scores of 4 or 5 were included in the "percent agreeing."

Source: BCG HBS Global Survey of 132 CEOs in 2001.

design of the board rests. Relying on tradition and habit in the modern boardroom must be reduced. By openly discussing and determining the board's role, its relationship with management, and the time it will commit to its tasks, directors will not diminish the board's enormous task, nor will they find more time to spend on it. But they will be able to develop the best possible way of managing it within their time and knowledge constraints. With this as a foundation, in chapter 5 we begin our examination of how boards can be designed to more effectively play their chosen role.

CHAPTER five

Structures That Work

"How can the chairman and chief executive roles be split? Can two jockeys ride the one horse?" — DIRECTOR

"How can the chairman and chief executive roles be combined? Isn't that like putting the fox in charge of the chickens?" — DIRECTOR

ONCE A BOARD HAS DECIDED WHAT ITS ROLE SHOULD be, the challenge becomes one of design. The structure of the board is a good place to begin. Given the job at hand, what structure will best allow the board members to perform to their maximum potential? What is the optimum board size? What is the best ratio of executive to independent directors? Should the chairman be the CEO, or should there be some other leadership arrangement? What committees should the board have?

Such questions already receive a great deal of critical scrutiny. In fact, board structure has become one of the great hopes of those concerned with improving corporate governance. For example, in its May 6,

2002, cover story on "The Crisis in Corporate Governance," all the improvements called for by *BusinessWeek* were structural in nature.[1] And it is easy to see why structure has achieved such prominence in demands for board reform. Structure is *visible,* and changes in structure are *measurable.* Institutional investors, shareholder groups, and other interested parties can see from annual reports and proxy statements whether the structure of a board has been changed to meet their desires.

But as we have said, the problem is that even though these third parties can observe the results of their activism, what they cannot see is even more important: what is actually taking place in the boardroom, and whether structural change has had any effect on the board's behavior. In achieving structural change, governance activists have the sound intention of solving a problem and setting the stage for stellar board performance going forward. In reality, they may simply have moved some pieces on the chessboard without being certain of their effect on the outcome of the game.

They also have no idea whether the directors believe the changes are valuable, or whether they have instituted them simply for appearances' sake. Consider the directors' dilemma. Board members may want to please those who call for improved structure, but if they do not also consider what such changes are going to do for their work, they are missing the real point of change. For any board to change its structure in a way that will truly support its role, the impetus—and the ensuing new structure—must come from within. *The directors themselves— with or without external pressure—must decide on the structure that will best allow them to do the job at hand well.*

As a General Rule . . .

WE'VE SAID that we believe there's no such thing as a universally applicable, ideal board structure. A particular structure that meets the unique needs of one board might be completely inappropriate for another. Indeed, top-performing companies around the world have a wide variety of governance structures, with different leadership models, very different ratios of insiders to outsiders, different board sizes, and varying committees. These structural differences have no apparent effect on the relative performance of the company or its board.

But as we pointed out in chapter 1, although we believe that boards must be designed to fit their circumstances and those of their company, we also have a point of view on what is likely to work best most of the time. Having helped many boards as they think through structural choices, we believe many of the proposed board innovations in the best practice paradigm do make sense for most boards.

For example, our own experience supports the notion that smaller boards are more effective than larger ones. This premise is also supported by a great deal of research into the functioning of decision-making groups. Smaller numbers of people are easier to involve in discussions, and such meetings are easier to lead.[2] (There are, of course, other factors to consider in thinking about board size, which we'll discuss later on in the chapter.)

We also endorse the idea that boards should consist predominantly of independent directors, though we believe, again, that there is no single "right" ratio of insiders to outsiders. We believe, further, that every board needs to provide clear leadership for the independent directors either by separating the jobs of chairman and CEO, or by establishing a "lead director." As we explain shortly, the appropriate choice depends upon the board's particular circumstances.

Finally, there is a widespread view that all boards should have at least three committees—an audit committee, a compensation committee, and a corporate governance committee—made up of independent directors.[3] Given the continuing concern about the integrity of accounting numbers, CEO compensation, and board oversight, we agree that such committees are essential for every board. However, we must recognize that virtually all companies in the English-speaking world had these committees in place throughout the 1990s and into the twenty-first century, generally led by non-executive directors, but we still had Enron, WorldCom, and a host of other accounting disasters, as well as unprecedented executive greed. It is clear that the mere presence of these committees does not provide the solutions we need. What matters is whether these committees achieve their purpose, which is something we'll discuss in more detail later on.

These are "our" general rules. But although we believe these best practices are sound for many boards, we cannot emphasize enough that an individual board's structural choices should no more be dictated by just these best practices than by past tradition or habit. Some boards will find that some of these best practices will indeed suit their needs. But others will find that no existing mold really does the job. If ever there was a time in the history of boards to "think out of the box," this is it. Hopefully, in the future, more boards *will* invent innovative designs of their own.

We should also note, before moving on, that we recognize that legal requirements in different jurisdictions may constrain a board's structure choices—for example, the requirement for dual boards in some European countries essentially dictates the leadership model to be adopted, a chairman of the management board and a chairman of the supervisory board. Similarly, in Germany, law prescribes the membership of the supervisory board. Despite such legal constraints, however, we believe that most boards around the world face similar structural choices.

One Size Does Not Fit All

BOARD SIZE provides a good starting point to discuss the need for individual boards to tailor their structural choices. While smaller boards have definite advantages over large boards, an individual board's circumstances should determine the appropriate number of directors. What factors should influence board size? A primary one is the skill set the board needs in order to do its job. Each board needs a specific range of skills and experience around the table.[4] The more categories of expertise directors feel they need to do their job, the larger the board will have to be.

Some proposals for board reform require boards to add certain types of members or take on new responsibilities. For example, the

Sarbanes-Oxley Act in the United States requires that all audit committees have at least one member with accounting or financial expertise. This necessitates that all publicly listed companies have at least one independent director with these qualifications on their board.

A second factor that affects board size is, quite simply, the efficient use of time. The directors of any large company often live in different cities, or even countries, and scheduling individual committee meetings can thus be a chore.

Given the time limits boards face, it's generally more efficient for all of the board's committees to meet simultaneously just prior to the full board's meetings. This means a board needs enough members so that there isn't any overlap among committee rosters.[5] For example, in the United States with all boards required to have three committees plus any discretionary committees, it is likely that the logistics involved in scheduling meetings is only going to get more complicated, and this may cause boards to seek more members.

We accept this reason for increasing board size, but we remain strongly committed to the proposition that boards should strive to be as small as they can be. What do we mean by "small"? If pushed to offer a number, we would suggest a maximum of ten directors. We believe eight to ten members are appropriate for some companies, and even fewer—perhaps six to eight—are sufficient for smaller or less complex companies, although with these smaller boards, scheduling committee meetings may be a problem. A very few companies might be able to justify larger boards—perhaps around twelve directors—but we find it hard to imagine a justification for a much larger number than that.

Some boards are exploring innovative ways to add specialist skills and meet the demands of time spent in committee without increasing total board size. A few, for example, are inviting a couple of nondirector outsiders to serve on board committees that deal with highly technical issues. The global resources company, BHP Billiton, has added several nondirectors with advanced scientific and technical skills to its environment committee. Qantas, the Australian airline, has added a former pilot to its board safety committee. In both cases, a board committee has gained deep expertise without adding to the total size of the board. And more than a few boards we know of have resigned themselves to allotting more time for committee meetings, so that they can accomplish their tasks without adding to their bulk. This is the choice we would recommend ourselves if the choice were between keeping the board small and efficient scheduling of committees.

Consistent with our views, board size has declined in recent years, although the average board on both sides of the Atlantic is larger than our ideal. Today, the average board of a larger U.S. company has twelve directors, down from around sixteen at the start of the 1980s, according to Spencer Stuart.[6] In Europe the average is around thirteen directors.[7] Needless to say, these averages conceal huge variations among companies and across countries. For example, U.S. banks average seventeen members, and some have more than twenty. Around 35 percent of S&P 500 boards still have more than twelve directors. And the average German board, at around twenty members, is more than twice as large as the average U.K. board.[8] This is because German law mandates boards of sixteen to twenty, depending on company size.

We are concerned that the trend toward smaller boards appears to be slowing. In fact, recent surveys show that many directors think their boards could grow and remain effective. According to an Egon Zehnder survey, North American and European directors believe that the maximum size for an effective board is about fourteen members.[9] More than half of the respondents to the 2000 Spencer Stuart Board Index believed that the ideal board should have between twelve and fourteen directors, and around 20 percent believe it should have fifteen or more.[10]

In spite of the view of these directors, we remain committed to smaller boards, and the CEOs in our survey agree. Over 70 percent agreed that boards of ten members or fewer are more effective, and this was the majority view across the regions as well (see appendix, Proposition E-3). As we said, our view is partly based on the basic precepts of group dynamics. Beyond a certain size, a board won't function well as a group. Large boards can breed inequality among the directors—in effect an "A" team and a "B" team develop because it becomes difficult for all directors to participate in discussions. Some directors on the "B" team even "go to sleep"—that is, they cease to contribute in any meaningful way, and they get away with such behavior because the pressure to be active and involved is minimal or nonexistent. In a large group, it is easy for individuals to assume that someone else will do a particular job. Think of the seventeen-member Enron board. Did the board's size provide more assurance for shareholders than a board half that size, in which each director might have felt a greater sense of responsibility?

If a board becomes larger, it can also become less powerful. That may seem counterintuitive, because a large board with many directors to oversee the CEO might appear more able to exercise its governance power. In practice, though, the reverse is more likely to be true. Consider the CEO who wants to control her board and starts by expanding its membership from ten to fifteen directors. Communication among directors would likely become increasingly difficult; directors would find it harder to get to know each other; a fraction of the board would be likely to participate in board discussions; and there would likely be little systematic contact among directors outside meetings.

What's more, if a director failed to prepare for a board meeting or to participate, the chances are that the lapse would go completely unnoticed.

To determine the right board size, directors must balance the need for group effectiveness, the need to carry out all the tasks required, and a schedule of time for committee meetings. Fortunately, these considerations don't always lead in different directions. The board's cohesion and working effectiveness can be maintained at up to around ten members. This usually provides enough directors with the requisite experience, and enough to perform the required committee tasks.

The Matter of Independence

A s D I S C U S S E D in chapter 3, board independence has powerfully shaped the governance agenda. Every aspect of a board's structure is now evaluated in light of this requirement. A non-executive director with anything resembling a conflict of interest may even come under pressure to resign. Audit, compensation, or corporate governance committees will be criticized if their members are not independent. In the United States all members of these committees must be independent. More and more the presence on a board of any executive other than the CEO is likely to be opposed.

In the current context, a board's independence is judged by just how many of its members appear to be independent. However, we believe the truly critical issue is the independence of the whole board. To understand what we mean, directors should ask themselves these three questions:

- Should any executive other than the CEO serve as a director?
- Should the former CEO stay on the board?
- Should all of the outside directors be genuinely independent?

Executive Directors?

Most companies in most parts of the world believe that the CEO should have a seat at the board table, whether or not he is also the chairman. We agree. The CEO, after all, has the best understanding of the company and its environment and should be a full and equal participant in the board's deliberations. In fact, few senior executives would take on the leadership of a company without a place on the board, unless legislation specifically excluded that possibility. The more difficult issue is whether senior executives besides the CEO should be on the board. Practice varies widely around the world, driven by tradition and, in some cases such as Germany, by legal requirements.[11] Today, for example, U.S. boards include very few executives other than the CEO. The average S&P 500 board has around twelve directors, of whom typically only one or two are managers.

In the United Kingdom, where the long-standing practice of appointing mostly executive directors to boards is now widely opposed by governance reformers and the investment community, there is a trend toward appointing more non-executive directors. Today, the average U.K. board is roughly split equally between executives and non-executive directors.[12] In Germany, while senior executives are not part of the supervisory board, other employees are elected to the board and share in its duties along with the shareholders' representatives.[13]

There is merit in both the arguments for and those against having senior executives other than the CEO on the board. On the positive side, executive directors can contribute to board discussions because they have a deep knowledge of the company and its businesses. They can share with the CEO the task of educating the independent directors about the business. Their presence reduces the need for the CEO to understand all the detail and also means that the independent directors get more than one perspective from management. It is clearly less likely that a CEO can mislead the board, intentionally or otherwise, when some of the directors are insiders who also have intimate knowledge of the company. Finally, the argument for having more than one member of management on the board gains weight as companies grow in complexity, since it may be important to have managers on the board who understand all aspects of the company.

The counterarguments are twofold. First, a board sometimes needs to talk about difficult issues, in particular businesses or management issues, and this is harder to do with executives at the table. Second, executives in a board discussion almost always stick to the position taken by the CEO. We have seen too many situations when management directors never contribute to meetings for fear of contradicting their boss, the CEO. As one independent director told us, "Executive directors waste a seat at the table. They always stick to the party line."

A damaging example of "party line" behavior surfaced during the Royal Commission examination into the collapse of the Australian insurer HIH, the largest corporate failure in Australian history. The chief financial officer was also a director of the failed company and was being cross-examined about why he hadn't informed the board about the dire state of the company's U.S. operations. In his response, he said that he had warned the CEO about the problem but that "Mr. Williams was chief executive and my boss. I expressed my view to him, we'd discuss it, he formed a strong view otherwise, and I just went along with it."[14]

Both the pro and con arguments hold true for some boards in some circumstances. So in considering how many and which executives should be on a board, a careful assessment must be made of not only the knowledge they bring to the board, but also the likelihood that they will actively participate in board meetings. If the CEO is like Delphi's J. T. Battenberg, whom we described in chapter 1, a few executives on the board can be a definite plus. They are not likely to be inhibited in expressing their opinions. On the other hand, if the CEO insists that his managers adhere to his line of thinking—and this is the practice in many companies—adding other executives to the board will achieve nothing and certainly will waste seats at the table.

We also believe it is a bad idea to appoint executives to the board as a reward for their hard work and past service. Even worse is the practice of offering a board seat as a consolation prize to a senior manager who has lost the competition to be CEO. The only good reason to elect any senior manager to the board is that he or she has the capacity, will, and autonomy to contribute to its work.[15]

Our conclusion about the issue of executive directors is partly about principle. We do want to be certain that the board, taken as a whole, is independent. But it is also about arithmetic. We are committed to smaller boards, and we believe that the majority of directors should be non-executives. This means that a nine-member board, for example, could include up to four executive directors, including the CEO, but it would be very difficult for the five non-executive directors to carry out all the required committee tasks. Further, with such numbers, we doubt a board could really be independent because the executive directors would have so much impact.

Former CEO on the Board?

Should the retiring CEO stay on the board? In some companies and some countries he generally does, sometimes as chairman.[16] This is almost always a bad idea. Why? The new CEO feels cramped by the presence of her predecessor. The former CEO is naturally committed to actions taken during his tenure. Skeletons are harder to drag from the closet because nobody, neither the new CEO, nor the directors, wants to embarrass the retired leader. Thus needed changes in company strategy or organization are difficult to discuss, and so are delayed or avoided entirely. We believe GE historically has had it just right. When a CEO retired, he also left the board. He was provided an office away from the company's headquarters and its boardroom, and never looked back. In all the fuss about Jack Welch's perks and after-retirement income in 2002, the critics lost sight of this essential fact.

The only exception to this rule might be those unusual companies that are very collegial and nonhierarchical in structure. For example, some of the publicly listed professional service firms have a long tradition of team leadership in which the CEO is "first among equals." The partnership-style management culture and decision-making processes in these organizations might make it easier for a former CEO to take another kind of place in the team, but not necessarily on the board.

We also know of positive situations in which a retired CEO has returned to a board after an absence of several years, and not as chairman. In those situations, the interval allowed the new CEO to place his stamp on the company. This arrangement makes sense in some circumstances, particularly in countries where director talent is in short supply or where detailed knowledge of the company is difficult for a board to acquire.

These rare exceptions aside, however, we believe that if there is a place at all for the retired CEO in his old business, it might be as a mentor or adviser to the new CEO—but only if she wants his advice as strongly as he wants to provide it.

Outside Directors Genuinely Independent?

We have no argument with the principle that a clear majority of directors should be independent by the definitions currently in use, but also believe it might at times be beneficial to have one or two non-executive directors who know a great deal about the business, even if they are conflicted in some respect. If such a person is added to a board, their position must be clearly understood and protocols developed to deal with any conflict that arises. Any potential conflicts should be stated in the proxy statement and understood by other directors. Further, the director in question should excuse himself from discussion of any matter where he would have a conflict.

The assumption in the push for boards made up almost entirely of independent directors seems to be that outsiders with conflicts can't be trusted to do the right thing. This view has undoubtedly been hardened in the wake of the high-profile company collapses in 2001–2002 in the United States, but it is unfortunate nonetheless because it will be achieved at a cost. The fact that some directors with possible conflicts of interest have acted improperly does not mean that shareholders will be better off if all directors with a deep knowledge of the business but a potential conflict cannot be added to any board.

A number of CEOs have told us that some of their most useful directors are those who have had experience in their industry value chain. The CEOs in our survey were divided on this issue, but even in the United States, the hotbed of independence, a sizable minority appears to share our view that it is not necessary for all directors (other than the CEO) to be independent (see appendix, Proposition E-2).

So far we have talked about independence in a quasi-legal sense, something that can be confirmed for an individual through examination of her past and present connections with the company. However, independence is also a psychological condition. To be genuinely independent, directors must not be beholden to the CEO—a particular risk in the United States, where the CEO also usually leads the board. This means directors should be selected and invited to stand for election through a process that is clearly "owned" by their fellow directors. They are joining the company's board, not the CEO's. The CEO should certainly meet board candidates, and his opinions should be considered in selecting new directors. However, the final decision must belong to the board, usually through its corporate governance committee, and candidates should be very much aware of that. As the GM board guidelines state:

The Board itself should be responsible, in fact as well as procedure, for selecting its own members. The Board delegates the screening process involved to the Committee on Directors' Affairs with direct input from the Chairman of the Board as well as the CEO.

The invitation to join the Board should be extended by the Board itself, by the Chairman of the Committee on Directors' Affairs (if the Chairman and CEO hold the same position), the Chairman of the Board and the Chief Executive of the Company.[17]

Another problem related to independence can arise when directors represent major shareholders. These directors can find themselves in a complicated position. As nominally independent directors, they are expected to represent the interests of all shareholders, but they also have a responsibility to the shareholder they specifically represent. While we know of few instances where the courts or others have commented on the independence of such directors, we believe the best course is for them to follow the same procedures as any other directors who have a potential conflict of interest. They should disclose the potential conflict and excuse themselves from the discussion in situations where there could be a conflict.[18]

To summarize, we agree that boards should be largely made up of both technically and psychologically independent directors. However, some boards may gain from electing a few directors whose backgrounds might lead to some conflicts of interest from time to time—members of management, representatives of major shareholders, former advisers, or people with industry-related experience. Such directors can bring relevant knowledge that can be different from the CEO's and that can be very useful to the independent members. Our caveat is that their position must be clearly understood and accepted by other board members, and procedures developed to deal with any conflicts that arise. Further, full disclosure must be made to the shareholders and public. Such steps should ensure the independence of the board as a whole while at the same time balancing the proportion of independent directors against the need to increase the board's understanding of the business. The board's leadership, a topic to which we now turn, also has an important effect on how the independence of the whole board is achieved.

Board Leadership

N O A S P E C T of board practice creates more debate than the question of whether the chairman and CEO roles should be separate or combined. Views on this differ even in the English-speaking world, where proponents are passionate in defense of their respective positions. What is remarkable, however, is that each side struggles even to understand how the other's model could possibly work. Most Americans can't imagine how a company can operate *with* shared leadership, while the British, Australians, and many Europeans have difficulty understanding how a CEO can also be chairman, leading the board that is supposed to oversee his performance. If you don't believe us, just invite a couple of U.S. CEOs to dinner with their British or Australian counterparts, and let the debate begin!

As boards consider the leadership structure that is best for their circumstances, they need first to consider the business culture of their home country. That culture creates certain expectations by CEOs and other senior executives that are unique to each country. In the United States, for example, it is almost impossible to bring in a new CEO without making him chairman as well. To do otherwise would signal to the outside world that he is not truly responsible for the leadership of the company. The CEO himself would feel like a second-class business leader among his peers. In the other countries we have mentioned, CEOs accept and understand that they are not to be chairman. Having only the one job is in no way a blot on one's reputation.

Whichever choice is made, a board's leadership structure has a major impact on the degree of independence the board is likely to maintain. If the CEO and chairman is the same person, and the independent directors do not have some other designated leader, even a board consisting entirely of independent directors will find it difficult to be truly independent. In this situation, the CEO/chairman will have control over the board's agenda, the information provided to directors, and the conduct of board meetings. Further, the independent directors may find it difficult to convene and conduct meetings alone. All of this stacks the power deck in the CEO/chairman's favor and can make it difficult for the board to maintain its independent stance.

If you think we're exaggerating, consider the difficulties encountered by the GM board in the early 1990s. In retrospect, it is clear that many of the "independent" directors were uncomfortable with their company's declining performance and the leadership of Roger Smith and Robert Stemple, but they had no forum to talk to each other, and no leader to bring them together. It required the dire threat of a reduction in the company's debt rating to get them to act and encourage John Smale to serve as their leader. Once this decision was made, Smale and his fellow directors were in a position to act.

Separating the chairman and CEO jobs seems, to many observers, the ideal structure to ensure board empowerment and independence. The chairman leads the board, and the CEO leads management and the company. This arrangement is very popular with corporate governance activists on both sides of the Atlantic. Many institutional investors in the United States have proposed its adoption, and the Cadbury Report in the United Kingdom also endorsed it, as did the more recent report by the Conference Board in the United States and the Higgs Report in the United Kingdom.[19] Furthermore, a recent survey of U.S. directors carried out by McKinsey found that almost 75 percent support the appointment of a lead director and a surprising two-thirds support splitting the CEO and chairman roles.[20] We shall return to the idea of a lead director shortly.

As always in business, however, things are never as clear-cut as they seem at first glance. Consider the words of this U.S. CEO who has had experience on boards on both sides of the Atlantic:

Europeans can't understand how we combine the role of CEO and chairman. I've seen the case of British Telecom, where there has been a sequence of chairmen and CEOs and ongoing poor performance, so it's not a panacea to have the separation of the two roles. It all depends on the relationship of the people. It can work either way.

Recent research in the United Kingdom supports this view, and shows furthermore that the tasks undertaken by the chairman and the CEO in that country vary widely from company to company.[21] Some U.K. chairmen are so active in the leadership of their companies that most Americans would see them as taking on the CEO role, with the nominal CEO acting as what Americans would label the chief operating officer. These chairmen are at the office daily and take a very active part in developing strategy, "advising" the CEO, and monitoring the business. At the other extreme, some British chairmen limit their activities to leading the board, and only show up at company headquarters when they need to take care of board affairs. In between the two extremes, British CEOs and chairmen divide the work in a variety of ways. Sometimes an older chairman, often the retired CEO, is an adviser and mentor to a new CEO. Sometimes the chairman is responsible for investor and external relationships in addition to board leadership, but the CEO is in every other respect the leader of the company.

This description of the U.K. situation, which is supported by our own experience in Australia, where the roles have long been split, demonstrates that even when the *principle* of separate chairman and CEO roles is accepted, the *practice* is so varied that one is forced to question whether the principle is worth fighting for. Yet, as we have said, the debate around this issue is fierce. We see it as an instance of theory fighting practice. The theory says that the chairman and CEO roles should be separate, but supporters of the combined role can point to the success of many corporations, particularly in the United States, with the combined role as evidence that the theory is wrong or irrelevant.

Nevertheless, the argument against the combined leadership model persists. Its essence is that a board's major responsibility is to monitor the performance of the CEO and the management group, and it doesn't take much imagination to realize that this can be tricky if the chairman and the CEO are the same person. But no matter how hard governance activists in the United States push the separation argument, U.S. companies are slow to accept it. As we have already seen, most S&P 500 corporations are headed by CEOs who also chair their boards, and according to one recent survey, the proportion of U.S. boards in which the CEO and chairman roles are separated fell from 19 percent to 10 percent in the five years to 2001.[22] Is there an argument to support the combined role? We believe so, in terms of both principle and practice.

First, the theoretical argument for a combined role recognizes that the board's mandate isn't confined to monitoring management's performance. Boards are not only policemen. As we have seen, they also make decisions. They are supposed to agree to strategy. They approve major capital expenditures, acquisitions, and divestitures. As such, the board is intertwined with management in the decision-making process. It's a short step from there to believing that a board's effectiveness is enhanced when its leader is intimately familiar with the business. If independent directors need to be told about complex issues and educated to the point where they can contribute to such decisions, having the CEO in the chair to do this makes sense. And what if, as we have observed on occasion when the two roles are separate, the chairman's understanding of the business is so limited that his management of the agenda means that the board consistently fails to examine the deep issues?

Second, while conventional wisdom holds that boards govern management, the reality is much more complex. As we shall discuss more fully in chapter 8, outside directors have difficulty being effective unless management wants them to be. The CEO, regardless of whether there is a separate chairman or not, can determine what the board learns about the business and whether the directors contribute in any meaningful way. The independent directors are very part-time; they depend on management cooperation to be effective. Unattractive as it may be to advocates of splitting the roles, combining the CEO and chairman's jobs acknowledges this realpolitik.

However, there is obviously a need to ensure that, with this structure, the board remains in charge and maintains its independence. For this to happen, we believe two things are necessary: First, there must be an attitude of independence among the directors. Second, there must be a "lead director." The lead director's primary duty should be to convene and lead meetings of the independent directors when this is desirable or necessary. These may be regular sessions for the independent directors to exchange views or evaluate the CEO's performance, or they may be extraordinary sessions to deal with crises that involve the CEO, or where the CEO has a conflict of interests. In some situations, the lead director may take on responsibilities like those of the chairman, such as creating the board agenda, or acting as a conduit between board members and the CEO. However, these duties should be added with care, because they can undercut the chairman's role and impair the relationship between other directors and the CEO. In the end, a lead director should facilitate the ability of the independent directors to govern, not impair it.

In the United States, GE created a "presiding director" for its board in late 2002.[23] The first occupant of the position was the company's longest-serving independent director, Andrew Sigler, who also chaired the compensation committee of the board. The intention in giving the position to a senior director and one who also chairs such an important committee seems to be to give the position plenty of clout with other directors and also management. The duties of the presiding director at GE will be to lead at least three board meetings each year without management present. He will also work with the chairman and CEO to select committee chairmen, set the agenda for board meetings, and lead the board's annual self-evaluation.

Clearly the directors at GE seem determined to provide leadership for the independent directors, which we applaud. However, we also worry that creating a lead director with such an extensive list of duties may undercut the chairman's role and impair the free flow of communication between the chairman/CEO and the other directors. If the lead director assumes too much power, he may complicate and even limit the ability of the other directors to work with the chairman/CEO and to govern. Creating the right job descriptions for the chairman and lead director in such situations requires careful attention to ensure the effectiveness of the whole board. In the end, this is where the power for effective governance must reside.

Perhaps 25 percent of the largest companies in the United States have publicly announced the appointment of such a lead director. We believe that many other boards have made similar appointments but without any public announcement—perhaps because some U.S. CEOs believe this would indicate they had less than full control of their companies' destinies. Some other U.S. boards have solved the problem of independent leadership by designating a committee head or long-serving director to undertake this responsibility without the formal designation of "lead director." In our view the title given to the role is less important than the fact that the board has a truly independent leader in addition to the CEO/chairman.[24] But today, it is not tenable that the role is undisclosed to the public. The company's shareholders and other stakeholders are entitled to know who is responsible for carrying out leadership tasks in the boardroom, as well as for the company.

The structure in which the chairman and CEO roles are separate seems great in theory but can be complicated in practice, because powerful people and their egos are involved. We have already mentioned instances where a board's effectiveness is diminished because its chairman doesn't understand enough about the business. We have also seen boards rendered ineffective and companies damaged because of persistent conflict between the chairman and the CEO. There are also instances in which the management team is distracted because of interventions by a chairman who feels responsible for managing the business. Of course there are many examples of boards and companies where this leadership model works extraordinarily well, where the chairman and CEO understand and agree about their respective roles. In these instances the chairman leads the board and the CEO leads management.

Thus we conclude that the separation of the two leadership jobs is not as easy in practice as it seems in theory. It really only works well when there is clear agreement and complementary responsibilities between the chairman and CEO. Further, practical experience also shows that the combined chairman/CEO structure can be very effective. Our position about choosing between the two structures is, therefore, pragmatic. Either model can work well, but problems are likely to emerge whatever approach is adopted. The secret to a successful leadership structure, whichever choice is made, is to anticipate potential problems and to design processes to compensate for them.

Boards aren't very good at anticipating problems with their leaders, and they are usually slow to establish processes to deal with problems after they emerge. Perhaps they don't like to concede that top managers and directors are fallible. Such an admission would be to accept the possibility of failure, and this might not match the self-image of business leaders at the peak of very successful careers.

But the likely problems aren't hard to identify. U.S.-style boards of independent directors led by the CEO/chairman can be slow to react to emerging business issues. This may be because the outside directors don't know each other well enough to mobilize and act. Or the CEO's control of the board agenda and the flow of information can leave them vulnerable. Perhaps the CEO is thin-skinned and reacts negatively if directors push hard for information. Or he might manage the meeting in a way that doesn't allow the outside directors to achieve the insight they need. On the other hand, where the roles are split, the chairman might intrude on the CEO's domain, resulting in a counterproductive clash of egos. Or the chairman might simply run the meetings and agenda in such a way that the board finds it hard to be truly effective. Even worse, the independent chairman might not adequately understand the business.

Every board should have a process or structure in place that provides a circuit breaker when problems like these arise. This should be the focus of design discussion, rather than excessive debate about the merits of the two leadership models. A prime example of what we have in mind is for every U.S.-style board to have a lead director. Where the leadership roles are separate, a board should also designate an independent director or perhaps the head of one of the board's committees, for example, the corporate governance committee, to monitor the working relationship between the CEO and the chairman on behalf of the board. This independent director should also provide the two company leaders and the board with feedback. Such a role is important because boards with split leadership are generally poor at providing feedback to errant chairmen.

The CEOs in our survey supported our view that some type of independent leadership is important. Support for the idea is predictably much lower in North America, but even here the views are almost evenly split rather than overwhelmingly opposed as we might have expected (see appendix, Proposition E-7).

Most governance activists do not concede the point that either leadership model can go awfully wrong, and continue to push U.S. companies to split the CEO and chairman roles. We'd suggest that they should be careful what they wish for. We believe their energies would be more productively directed toward ensuring that every board, regardless of its leadership structure, has a leader for the independent directors and an agreed procedure to deal with any leadership problems that arise. Without this, boards, whatever their leadership model, are likely to respond too slowly to leadership problems, with destructive effects on their companies.

As this discussion illustrates, the debate about the "best" leadership structure proceeds without any reference to the role a board intends to undertake. We are convinced that either leadership model is workable, whatever role a board chooses. However, it is also clear that the more active and involved a board becomes (like a pilot), the more important it is for the directors and management to have a clear understanding of their respective roles. Further, in such situations the board must have the knowledge to participate in decisions. If the chairman and CEO are different individuals, this means that the chairman must have a good grasp of the issues involved in major decisions and be certain the board has the relevant information. If the same individual holds the two positions, it may become incumbent on the lead director to ensure that management is forthcoming with the appropriate information, and that his fellow directors are comfortable with the information they are receiving, and that he personally understands the issues involved. This can increase the time and effort required of him.

If the board accepts more of a monitoring role (the watchdog), the distinction between the board's job and that of management is likely to be clearer. Further, whichever leadership structure is in place, the board will need to be assured that it has the appropriate procedure and information to perform its oversight function. Again, the responsibilities for this will fall to the chairman on the one hand or the lead director on the other.

Board Committees

T HE RATIONALE for establishing board committees is to divide up the work among board members so that they can accomplish more in their limited time. Committees allow directors to develop specialized understanding and to delve more deeply into specific issues. They are, in fact, the one example of where directors have been willing to divide up their work.

Most of the discussion around committees concerns the membership of the three core ones—audit, compensation, and corporate governance. Audit and compensation committees, in particular, have attracted a great deal of attention in the wake of high-profile accounting problems and unbridled CEO compensation. These committees are mandated in a growing number of jurisdictions, and there is broad agreement about their duties.[25] Surveys show that almost all companies in Europe, North America, and Australia have both audit and compensation committees.[26] In addition, an increasing number of Australian, European, and North American boards also have nominating or corporate governance committees, and this is now required in the United States. This committee manages the board's internal affairs, including the selection and nomination or renomination of board members, determining board composition, and assessing the overall effectiveness of the board. Today's best practice governance principles demand that every member of these core board committees be an independent director, and again this is required in the United States.[27]

Obviously, committees whose tasks are to monitor management (audit), appoint those who do the monitoring (corporate governance), and establish management compensation (compensation) should not contain management members. Management is inevitably involved in the work of these committees, but it is important to explicitly restrict management's role to providing information to these committees. In the end, it is essential that these committees make their decisions without any influence by management.

We know of instances in recent years where the CEO has formally stepped off these committees for appearances' sake only—to earn a tick of approval from those who measure good governance from the outside. No one should fool themselves into thinking formally eliminating the CEO or other managers from these committees will make a big difference by itself. It is too easy for them to insinuate themselves into committee deliberations by the information and advice they provide.

The best way to ensure effective and independent committees is to select a committee chairman who is not only an independent director in the technical sense, but one who has personal independence and integrity. A chairman is needed who not only has the knowledge of accounting, compensation, or corporate governance, but who also has the personality to stand up to any pressure from the CEO or others.

It is also important to think carefully about the size of committees and the procedures for selecting their members. While we have seen committees with as many as six members (e.g., the audit committee at Enron), we can see no reason for such large committees. In our experience, a committee of three members seems ideal (including the chairman). It is large enough to provide different perspectives, but small enough to reach decisions. Further, the "odd" number of members creates a certain healthy tension that can stimulate discussion about controversial issues.

Another advantage of such a small membership is that it can, and should, be used to encourage all members to become actively involved in the committee's work. Too often we have seen committee chairmen do all the heavy lifting while the other members only attend meetings and occasionally contribute to discussions. In an era when committees are being required to take on increased workloads (e.g., audit committees in the United States[28]), it is important for all members to share the work. In fact, we believe one of the hallmarks of effective committee chairmen is that they encourage all members to share the work, rather than doing it all alone.

We also advocate that committee chairmen and membership be rotated every few years, so that all board members serve on more than one committee during their tenure on a board and can learn about their company from that experience.

Board committees are subparts of the board, and all board members should share the responsibilities for all of them. We recognize that the provisions of the Sarbanes-Oxley Act (which gave greater responsibility to the audit committee to recommend the auditors to shareholders, to oversee auditors, etc.) make the audit committee independent of the rest of the board. Our concern is that this could disconnect that committee from board members who do not serve on it. However, we also believe that this new law notwithstanding, the board itself (usually through its corporate governance committee) has the right to select and rotate board members through the audit committee, as long as the members have the requisite knowledge. This fact, we believe, can be used to prevent too much separation of this committee from the board as a whole. Rotating members on this and other committees should ensure board cohesion.

Another major question is whether to establish additional committees beyond the three just described. In making decisions about this, there are two key issues: avoiding the board's intrusion too far into management's domain, and being certain that the creation of additional committees does not prohibit all directors from focusing on major issues. Let's look at each.

Because board committees are meant to be active and pursue issues in depth, it is possible that an additional committee (e.g., a strategy committee or a technology committee) may lead the directors on it to get involved in management's decisions. We have seen such board committees in operation and observed that they often create tension with management. The directors on such a committee can easily begin to second-guess and interfere with management, and this is usually a bad idea.

The second danger is that creating such committees will cause some directors to be left out of important decisions. Strategy is perhaps the perfect example. While there have been calls for and attempts to create strategy committees, most boards have resisted the idea. They believe, as we do, that all the directors should contribute to discussions about significant strategic questions. If a committee is formed to focus on strategy or similar major issues, the involvement of the board as a whole will be reduced. Given that the board is created in the first place to reflect the broad perspective needed to govern the company, all its members should be deeply involved in discussions of such major issues.

But boards do have a huge task, and as we argued in chapter 3, it is necessary to divide up some of the work if the job is to get done. Thus, we see a place for discretionary board committees that meet a company's specific needs. This might include committees that oversee areas of major risk, particularly where there is threat of massive legal liability or where a mistake could sink the company. For example, many resources and chemical companies create environment committees, because a serious mistake in this area could have catastrophic consequences. Similarly, financial institutions add risk committees and airlines have safety committees. Any business exposed to huge risk that could quickly destroy it can make a case for a specialist board committee to focus on that risk.

While some directors could argue that some of these issues are so important that the whole board should handle them, boards struggle to do the job well when deep technical issues are involved. Think about it. Everyone acknowledges that the matters considered by the audit committee are crucially important, but most people understand that this is specialist territory, best handled by a committee that can achieve real focus on the issues that matter. The risk of the "whole board" approach on complex matters is that in theory every director is involved, but in practice no one takes responsibility; it is simply too difficult for all the directors to understand the technical details.

Committees can also signal to employees and other stakeholders that certain matters are crucially important to the company. For example, Medtronic, mentioned earlier, has created a technology and quality committee that clearly demonstrates the board's interest in these matters. Because the committee members have technical or scientific backgrounds, they can interact with and earn the respect of the company's technical community. The existence of this committee also underlines the critical importance of product quality and the need to follow all quality procedures. No risks can be taken with product quality, because failure to follow appropriate procedures could result in a criminal indictment for senior managers, not to mention being life-threatening to patients.

Specialist territory aside, our position is that there should be few permanent committees beyond the three core ones. But we do advocate temporary ad hoc committees to enable a few directors to involve themselves in-depth on specific topics that are important to the board at particular times. These might include an acquisition or divestiture of an ailing or noncore business. The lack of progress in R&D might be causing concern. Executive development or management succession might be seen as a challenge. Most crucial of all, there might be a need to search for, and select, a new CEO.

The board of Lukens Steel provided an example of the use of such a committee in 1991.[29] It was considering the acquisition of Washington Steel, another producer of specialty steel. The decision was of major significance for Lukens, so it was decided to create an ad hoc committee, labeled the "Melter's Committee," to review all the due diligence information used by management and its bankers, lawyers, and consultants in proposing the transaction. The five members of the committee then held a meeting with senior management to ask questions and to assure themselves that management's recommendation was sound and based on careful analysis. The committee concluded that this was indeed the case, recommending the acquisition to the full board, which agreed.

In the United States, the Delaware courts have called for the establishment of temporary committees labeled "special committees" to make recommendations to the full board in the event of a leveraged buyout offer from management. In these instances, the key idea is "to unwrap the bindings that have joined the directors into a single board," so the independent directors on the committee can make a truly independent judgment about what is in the best interest of shareholders without regard to what inside directors want.[30] We believe that the use of such committees of disinterested directors are a sound idea for any major matter in which management may have a strong interest and which the board wishes to study independently. In all these cases, the ad hoc committee's task is to analyze the matter intensely and to make a recommendation to the full board so that it can make the most carefully thought out and informed decision.

While temporary committees can be a good way for directors to become more deeply involved in important issues, they should be established with clear sunset clauses, so that they do not become institutionalized, become an irritant to executives, or lead to excluding the board as a whole from important matters.

Finally, one traditional committee that still exists in many companies—the executive committee—should be critically examined. Almost every board used to have such a committee, usually made up of the chairman, the CEO, and a few other experienced directors. The rationale was that, if important matters needed attention between scheduled board meetings, the executive committee could handle them, later reporting its decisions to the full board. Today we think executive committees are usually a *bad* idea because they lead to the creation of "A" and "B" teams on the board. Directors who are on the executive committee are in on critical matters; the rest are not. Thus, the very existence of the committee can be divisive. Fortunately, technology has made such committees redundant. When a matter urgently requires board action, it's now possible to quickly convene a telephone meeting of the whole board.

Designing Board Structure

As the discussion in this chapter reveals, boards are most likely to be effective if their structures are designed to suit the circumstances of their company and the role the board has elected to play. Although there are a few generalizations about board structure that are widely accepted and with which we essentially agree (small is better, independence is essential, either leadership structure can work, three core committees), individual boards must build on these basic ideas to create the unique structure they require. There are no simple rules for doing this, but there are a few key questions boards can ask themselves that will illuminate and clarify the issues:

- How do we balance the need for independent directors with the requirement for a knowledgeable board? What mix of independent, nonindependent outside directors, and management directors do we need to sustain board independence while making sure that the board is informed and knowledgeable?

- What leadership structure will work best—contributing to independence and producing the desired behavior—a combined chairman and CEO with a lead director, or a separate chairman and CEO? Regardless of the choice made, what can go wrong, and what procedures should be put in place to deal with potential problems?

- What permanent committees does the board need? How will chairmen and members be selected? When and how should temporary committees be used to engage directors more fully in issues that are pressing at the time?

If a board seeks answers to these questions in light of its circumstances and desired role, it can design a structure that will facilitate its work. In some instances, the solution may be at variance with the conventional wisdom about best practices. However, as should be clear by now, we are less concerned about boards adhering strictly to the standard of best practices than we are that they are designed to encourage the behavior that will lead to their effectiveness.

Building and Sustaining
the Right Team

"It is really hard to find good directors."

—BOARD CHAIRMAN

"It is really hard to get rid of poor performers on the board."

—INDEPENDENT DIRECTOR

WHILE BOARD STRUCTURE IS IMPORTANT AND IS the best place to begin thinking about board design, in our judgment the caliber and abilities of the directors is an even more critical determinant of a board's effectiveness. Good people—and people who are suited to the job at hand—will perform well even if the structure is less than ideal, but the opposite is certainly not true. Even with a perfect structure, modest talent, or expertise that isn't suited to the needs of the company, will limit a board's effectiveness. In this chapter we examine how to bring together the right team of people and how to sustain that team once it is assembled.

Changing the quality of a typical board's membership has traditionally been a slow and very difficult process. Most of the new faces on boards, even today, appear because existing members have reached retirement age or tenure limits. Deadwood persists because boards typically have had a hard time getting rid of subpar performers. Directors simply have found it very difficult to face up to noncontributing peers. They are colleagues, often long-standing ones, and it is difficult to ask such people to resign. Further, very few boards have any concept of offering education and development for their members (or much motivation to do so). So even those board members who would otherwise grow into their roles in an exemplary way if given the right kind of training are at a disadvantage. The assumption is that every director knew all she needed to know before joining the board and can now dispense that wisdom at the boardroom table.

The difficulty of improving the quality of board members is exacerbated by a perceived shortage of good, qualified directors. Everyone wants the same few people, who are almost always older men with substantial management experience. Everyone seems to want prominent CEOs or people who were recently CEOs of major corporations. But do the math: There are more than ten board seats for each CEO position; if this is the only talent pool from which directors are sought, there is always going to be a shortage of talent.

How can boards get past these ingrained mind-sets and established practices? By overhauling the entire process of seeking, nominating, and developing directors.[1] Put simply, boards—along with managers, shareholders, analysts, and other stakeholders—need to think differently about the type of people who make good directors and about how they are encouraged to live up to their potential once on the board. Specifically, they need to:

- *Widen the talent pool.* Think more broadly than about just current and former CEOs. For example, widen the age and experience criteria to add younger but experienced executives as board members.

- *Think strategically about the skill mix,* particularly in light of the challenges facing the business and the board's agreement about

its role. Gather the skills and experience that the board specifically needs to oversee its company.

- *Raise the performance bar*. Develop a performance culture in
  the boardroom. The corporate governance or nominating committee should review the performance of each director who is
  being considered for renomination to be certain they meet the
  board's criteria for performance. This will make renomination
  more than a formality, and provide a realistic way to remove
  underperforming directors.

- *Insist on an education process for new directors*. And regularly
  refresh the existing directors. Help them to keep up with rapid
  change by educating them about the company's changing
  environment. Help them to learn and stay excited about the
  business.

- *Be realistic about compensation*. Cultivate professionalism
  rather than greed, while making it worthwhile for board members to put in the required effort.

At first glance, these seem like obvious solutions. But as anyone
who has ever served on a board knows, group dynamics, history, and
tradition act as powerful restraints that can frustrate even the smallest
change efforts, let alone a full-scale campaign to change who serves on
a board, how they get there, and how they serve once they're on the job.

Let's discuss each of our recommendations in detail.

Widen the Talent Pool

M OST OF THE TIME, when boards discuss the talent that sits
around the table, the talk inevitably centers on CEOs. Whether
they make great directors because of their previous management experience. Whether they make lousy directors because they can't adjust to
an environment where theirs is not necessarily the most important
opinion and where they must listen more than they talk. How some of
them can't seem to understand a business they haven't experienced.

How others want to get more into management's territory than their job as director requires.

Headhunters who specialize in board appointments also report that the typical request for a new director starts with the assumption that the best directors are present or past CEOs. As one told us:

> Board clients want someone who is or has recently been a CEO of a major and successful business. Someone with a good grasp of technology would be a bonus, as would experience running a global business. And yes, a woman or a representative of a prominent minority would be great.

We think that a lot of the discussion about the ideal director's qualifications misses the point. Most CEOs argue that CEOs make the best directors, as did those in our survey (see appendix, Proposition E-1). Most non-CEOs argue the opposite. That's understandable—a CEO has a sound understanding of what he brings to the boardroom table, but for him the contribution a non-CEO could make is likely to be less convincing or more of an unknown. And vice versa. Both sides are arguing rationally, from their perspectives, but they are debating the wrong issue.

What if the issue was framed another way—say, for example: "What personal qualities and talents do you want in an outstanding director?" We might find more agreement in that case. The question of a director's prior occupation could then be seen as an important but secondary issue rather than the central point of the debate. Put simply, we think the CEO versus non-CEO debate is unhelpful.

In that spirit, then, we suggest that board members should first agree about the fundamental qualities that every director needs. Here's what we believe the six essentials are.

- *Intellectual capacity:* Can the prospective director understand a business in which she has no experience? Is she smart enough to see what really drives performance? As we have just said, many very successful executives can't think their way into a business in which they've never worked. They just wheel out the solutions that worked for them. The work of a board is highly cerebral—intellectual capacity is a must.

- *Interpersonal skills:* Can the prospective director work as part of a group? Does he listen well? Can he express his views in ways that are both challenging to and supportive of management? People who have been successful in their business or profession can face a difficulty here. By the time they reach the age at which most directors join boards, they are accustomed to expressing their own opinions and too often expecting others to fall into line. They aren't necessarily skilled at listening to and reaching agreement with "equals." This is a problem—good directors are good listeners and effective communicators, and can relate to other board members as peers.

- *Instinct:* Does the prospective director have good business instincts and judgment? This isn't the same as intelligence. It's about "making a dollar." It's about street smarts and commercial acumen. Faced with strategic and organization decisions, can the candidate sense where the value lies and what issues might stand in the way of achieving this value? Can she quickly get to the heart of such issues?

- *Interest:* Is the prospective director genuinely interested in the company, its business, and its people? Does he have the commitment to go the extra mile when necessary? Since serving as a director is usually not about making a lot of money, is he passionate enough about the business to remain engaged and committed over a period of several years?

- *A commitment to contribute:* Is the director too busy to be seriously engaged? We disagree with arbitrary rules that limit the number of boards on which a director can serve, because "busyness" in life derives from many other factors. The important question is this: Will she—can she—enthusiastically put in the time needed?

- *Integrity:* Directors must be truthful and honest. Will the prospective director accept accountability for his role in decisions? Will his priority be to do what is right for the company rather than protect his own position and reputation?

Boards that perform badly usually have members with deficiencies in many of these areas. Too many directors might struggle to understand the business and its risks. Or they might not be very good at creating a discussion that illuminates the important issues. Perhaps they are too busy to pay enough attention. Such failings cannot be linked to occupational background. We know that some CEOs and former CEOs will have the attributes we are describing, while others will not, and the same will be true for directors who are not CEOs. Corporate governance committees should focus on attributes like these rather than whether a candidate is or is not a CEO.

Oddly enough, most CEOs responding to our survey share the view that boards need to have more diversity among their membership (see appendix, Proposition C-9). The problem is that to date, discussions of diversity too often are mere blips on a radar screen that is primarily focused on the CEO ranks.

Think Strategically About the Mix

WE ARE NOT ARGUING for diversity for its own sake. Rather, we want the selection process to find potential directors who have diverse expertise and experience that fits the specific needs of the company.

Identifying this expertise and experience must come after the decision about the board's role. In chapter 4, we described the way a board should seek to achieve the appropriate mix of oversight, decision making, and advice to management. The selection of new directors for a board should obviously reflect these decisions.

To be more concrete about how boards should think about their composition, let's assume that we are considering a board for a global consumer products company that has defined its role to be seriously engaged in the important issues facing the company (a pilot board).

Let's also assume that we want ten directors—small enough to work effectively, but large enough to give the mix of skills needed and to staff the board's committees. In reality, of course, we would be unlikely to have the opportunity to create an "ideal board" such as this from scratch. But directors must fill board places from time to time, and this is the opportunity to make a real difference. To build the best possible board, directors must consider two matters: the skills and experience needed going forward, and the skills and experience of the existing directors. This comparison will put the focus onto emerging gaps in experience and specific skills, and drive the discussion toward informed agreement on the sorts of people the board really needs to add. In doing this, an analogy to sports teams is helpful. Good teams are not simply collections of the best available individuals. Great coaches don't just pick the best players; they build teams with the understanding that each player has a specific job to do.

And so it is with boards. Different directors have different skills, and we believe that boards are more effective if the appropriate mix of skills is explicitly selected and recognized. We understand the historical reasons for the view that directors like to think of themselves as interchangeable parts (jointly responsible for everything), but we think this view can make them gifted amateurs at all aspects of the board's work. Classic generalists are suboptimal board members in an increasingly complex business world.

Those who want to design effective boards must recognize that they need directors with different abilities. Some are good at finance, others understand marketing, while one is familiar with business practices in China. The key goal in selecting directors is to build a mix of experiences that is appropriate to the board's needs. Recognizing such strengths does not mean those with less knowledge in a specific area are relinquishing their responsibility. Rather, they are trusting the judgment of colleagues with more experience in that area. So, with these principles in mind, let's visit "central casting" and consider what mix of skills and experience we would want for this board.

We'll begin with an obvious choice. The CEO must be on the board unless laws preclude it.[2] Even if she is not a board chairman, she should be on the board because she is the driver of the board's agenda and the key informant to the board about the company. Further, as we will point out in chapter 8, the relationship between the CEO and the board will be strongest if the CEO and the board see each other as partners.

We then need to find at least two or three directors—whose strength, to be frank, is to keep the other board members and management out of trouble. This is because some of the board's responsibility involves difficult accounting, financial, and legal matters in a context where violation of laws or regulations is a constant risk. Further, in some companies, there might be serious environmental or other risks. A major error in these circumstances could have catastrophic results for the company and therefore for its directors.

So every board should have at least one or two directors who really understand the numbers: the financial reporting and all of the complex accounting issues. They will happily apply pedantic intensity to the audit committee's work. Given the right personal qualities, a former or active CFO would be a promising candidate. In the United States, boards are now required to have at least one audit committee member with accounting or financial expertise.

We would also seek a director or two with experience in other areas of major risk that could sink the company, as well as the tools for managing them. For example, our company might deal in food products, which carry a health risk. Or it could be a financial risk, because as a global company we have complex currency exchange risks. (We actually know of bank boards where not a single director has hands-on experience in today's hugely complex financial markets—a big mistake.) Ideally these directors will also have strong operations experience. They might, for example, have run a business division in a noncompeting consumer product company or been head of the treasury operations in a global company.

We have now filled three or possibly four slots. Next, we'll look for directors with good track records as CEOs, either in the recent past or currently. While as we said earlier, we don't want to overload the board with CEOs, we do want a few on the board. Each board should include directors who know what it is like to lead an organization, articulate a vision, manage change, understand the loneliness of top leadership, and deal with the media and financial markets.

In seeking these CEOs, relevant experience in companies like ours that market to consumers would be ideal. Since our business is global, we would prefer CEOs with experience in running a company across national boundaries. As a public company, we will want CEOs with experience in running such companies and dealing with the pressure of capital market expectations.

Next we want one or two additional members who are not necessarily CEOs, but who also have experience in consumer products. Successful candidates are likely to have had high-level executive experience leading major divisions in large companies.[3] If we are an automobile manufacturer, for example, we will search for someone with strong experience somewhere in the auto industry value chain. The right candidate will ideally have a deep interest in how the whole industry is developing and changing. If we are a food manufacturer, we might look for someone with leading-edge experience in food retailing, agribusiness, or consumer marketing. And if we find a candidate who has these qualities but also has some potential conflict of interest, we might accept this and develop procedures to ensure probity. As we argued earlier, boards must consider the trade-off between "independence" and "knowledge."

We recognize that corporate governance activists and some directors would dispute our view that a board might include members with industry or functional skills that closely relate to the businesses of the company. Many senior executives also believe the presence of such directors simply replicates management expertise (and life *can* be more comfortable without too much challenge from the board). But we believe a good board must be able to offer contestable advice and smell any smoke coming under the door. This requires some members with experience relevant to the industry. So we want one or two outside directors who are broadly knowledgeable about our main businesses. However, we also want them to be "big picture thinkers" who will not become enmeshed in the details and create conflicts with senior management.

Other specific skills may be required—around, for example, functions, geographies, or customer segments. If our company is making a huge commitment to Asian markets, we want to find a director who has already walked that path. If we are making substantial technology investments, or depend on the strengths of our consumer brands or R&D efforts, we want to find directors who have such experience. If our business deals extensively with government regulation, we might want to consider a former public servant or politician who understands the regulatory process.

By now we have seven or eight candidates. We will add a director who has experience in developing corporate strategy. One of our board's primary duties will be to appraise and approve the company's strategy, a task that requires skill and judgment born out of deep experience in a very wide variety of industries. This is likely to lead us to someone with strong experience in strategy work in one or more large global companies.

For our next director, in a company marketing to consumers, we want to include a business leader who can also constructively understand our business in the light of wider community attitudes. Businesses need social legitimacy to prosper, and we all know of companies paying dearly for their neglect of such concerns. Recent cases include Nike with low-paid workers, Shell in Nigeria, Monsanto with genetically modified crops, and a number of pharmaceutical companies with the cost of AIDS drugs in Africa. Boards and their executives are mostly from the same school—an understanding of grassroots activism is unlikely to be their strong point.

In looking for this person, we would ideally seek someone who understands business but who is familiar with life in the broader community. How many of our directors have any meaningful contact with the lives that most of our customers lead? How many have any appreciation of how a customer earning less than the national average income might react to changes in our company's price and service offering? How many regularly shop for our products? Empathy with the concerns of the wider population is a good attribute in a director.

Have we gathered enough in the way of experience and skills? We've probably gone as far as we can. No board can be expert in everything that might be relevant to the company's success—and we can't keep adding directors in an attempt to achieve that. But looking at the board we have put together, we see a balanced, diverse group of directors with some very clear categories of skills and experience that match the needs of our hypothetical company and its board.

It will not always be possible to construct such an "ideal" board. In some parts of the world there is very clearly a shortage of experienced talent. Our advice in this situation is to seek directors who have relevant skills and knowledge, although a smaller pool will mean that these boards may be less likely to include CEOs and may have more former public servants, academics, and others with nonbusiness experience. The most important need in these parts of the world is to get directors who have strong accounting and financial expertise, as well as integrity. Publicly listed companies in developing countries have to work very hard to convince global investors that their boards are capable of taking an independent view. To have any chance of this at all, they must first appoint directors of unquestionable reputation to key roles such as the audit committee.

Much of the discussion about board membership focuses on the topic of gender and ethnic diversity, and the very low representation of women and minorities on boards, so we cannot conclude this discussion without declaring our point of view. We agree that it's important to address these issues. Having said that, we are wary of tokenism. Every board seat is important; there's no room for a director who doesn't possess, at the minimum, the six essential attributes we listed earlier.

We also believe that the so-called shortage of board talent among women and many ethnic minorities is the logical outcome of the view that the only good directors are CEOs and ex-CEOs—and we note that 99 percent of the CEOs of S&P 500 companies in 2002 were male.[4] But as we have already explained, we don't accept the premise. There is room on a good board for directors who haven't been CEOs, and a logical step is to look to those business professions where women and minorities are already well represented.

To summarize, it's possible to build a diverse and effective board, but only if companies widen the talent pool and search for directors who will contribute to the mix of abilities that fit the board's need. We believe the often-mentioned shortage of candidates is more likely to reflect nominating committees' failure to look beyond the obvious than it is because of a genuine lack of talent.

Raise the Performance Bar

T RADITIONALLY, once directors were elected to a board, they tended to serve on it until they reached a retirement age, or in some cases, until it was embarrassingly obvious that they were no longer mentally able to serve. In essence, most boards have not had performance standards for directors. Board surveys indicate that this is still too often true. Very few boards ever ask a member to resign or not to stand for reelection.[5] Our experience is that few boards remove poor directors, and the CEOs in our survey agree (see appendix, Proposition E-5). Every time we work with a board, we are told it is difficult to remove a director who is not pulling his weight. No one wants to be critical of a longtime colleague. If a football team operated on the same principle, it's not difficult to imagine what the outcome would be. We believe that boards should learn a lesson from team sports, where mediocre players are dropped and even those who are successful are sometimes moved on to rebalance the skill mix on the team.

Poor performance on a board can be the result of several factors. Although the trend is for boards to work harder than they did in the past, not all directors can or want to put in the required effort. And some simply don't bring anything new to board discussions—a failing that might reflect lack of effort or simply that they have nothing to contribute. Some directors who once made important contributions lose interest or become too busy to continue to contribute at the level they once did.

Whatever the reason, when a director's performance is an issue, it's clear that boards must raise the performance bar. Unchallenged tenure of a decade or more is a luxury that no longer can be justified. Recognizing that directors do not like to sit in judgment of their peers, we offer several suggestions to deal with what is clearly a thorny issue.

Performance Reviews at Renomination

Each director is elected for a defined term, usually two or three years, and then renominated for another term, and perhaps another and another. While such renomination and reelection by the shareholders has been automatic in the past, we believe that the renomination is a perfect time for there to be an honest assessment of each director's performance. The board committee responsible for selecting directors (the corporate governance or nominating committee) should carry it out. This idea is gaining increasing acceptance as part of best practices, although as recently as five years ago such reviews were rare. Directors were seen as being above any evaluation. For example, the Higgs Report in the United Kingdom in 2003 reported that "over three-quarters of non-executive directors and over half of chairmen have never had a formal personal performance review."[6] The rationale for nonreview was that directors were accountable only to shareholders, who would exercise their judgment in annual general meetings. But this argument is specious, since shareholders routinely approve the slate of directors that the board nominates. The underlying problem was that directors did not want to evaluate each other.

Nearly half the leading companies in the English-speaking world now carry out some type of board performance reviews, although European and Asian companies have yet to tackle the issue in a serious way.[7] As positive as this seems, the fact remains that most of these reviews focus on the whole board, and not on individual directors.

The 2001 Korn/Ferry survey of U.S. directors indicated that, while only 19 percent of respondents reported that they were evaluated on an individual basis, 71 percent believed that they should be.[8] Perhaps this reflects a generational shift on boards, with the appointment of new directors long accustomed to evaluation and feedback in their executive careers who realize that their performance as directors should be evaluated as well. Performance appraisal for individual directors, as well as boards, is an idea whose time has come.

An evaluation of directors at the time of renomination assures shareholders that those being renominated have been performing well.

The risk that highly capable people are removed only because they offended management is reduced when the non-executive directors make the decision. It is appropriate to make these directors responsible for monitoring the quality of their own team and recommending their candidates to the shareholders. Any director who believes his removal is unjustified can always choose to expose the matter for public debate.

We believe the process of evaluating individual directors should start with a director who is up for renomination preparing a statement of self-evaluation indicating his contribution to the board. The corporate governance committee should then decide whether they agree with this self-assessment or whether they believe there is a gap between their view of the director and the way he sees himself. The committee next should check with other board members to understand whether its views are shared. If there are broad concerns about a director's performance, the committee must decide whether to recommend against renomination or for renomination with an agreement with the director as to how she will modify her behavior to reach her colleagues' expectations. Whichever decision is made, it is the responsibility of the chairman of the committee and the chairman of the board to provide appropriate feedback to the director involved.

Turning to the evaluation of the board as a whole, we believe it is an absolutely essential requirement for every board. Why such a strong feeling? As we have pointed out several times, a major problem for boards is tradition and inertia. One way to overcome this is to conduct an evaluation of the way board members, as well as members of senior management, perceive the way the board is doing its job and how all involved feel about the board's understanding of its role as well as its composition, processes, and structure. In our experience, such an evaluation is the best antidote to boardroom inertia.

The process can be simple, but it should also be structured. One approach is to use a written questionnaire. This should be given to the directors and senior executives who work closely with the board. The chairman or lead director or the corporate governance committee might create and administer the questions, but some boards find it helpful to use an outside facilitator. Many such questionnaires have been developed and are in the public domain.

Such evaluations can also be conducted by interviewing the directors as well as the managers who work with the board. The interviews are then summarized, and the consensus view presented to the board. The interviews can be conducted by an outside facilitator or by the lead director, board chairman, or the corporate governance committee. While the questionnaire approach has the advantage of allowing things to be quantified and thus can be compared to the results of any evaluations that preceded it, the interview approach can be more probing. Of course, by using a questionnaire supplemented by interviews, it is possible to get the advantages of both approaches.

The sort of process just described not only provides data about the board's performance, but also ensures that any important issues about an individual director's performance are put on the table—albeit indirectly. For example, if a director is often unprepared, rarely participates in board discussions, has a poor attendance record, or is not constructive in his contributions, it will show up in the overall evaluation as a weakness in the board. The director may not be identified by name, but everyone will almost certainly know who it is. In this way, the "whole board evaluation" provides a vital "data point" that a chairman, lead director, or corporate governance committee needs to take action. And when an errant director sees the questionnaire results, he may realize that "he is it" and either lift his game or begin to think about leaving before the heat goes up.

Finally, we don't believe that boards need to evaluate their performance annually. Every two years is about right. Boards don't meet that often, and annual reviews tend to run into one another and to absorb too much of the board's time. A new cycle begins as soon as last year's effort is finished. This can become tiresome, and people will begin to see evaluation as an endless process, which erodes its effectiveness. But that said, good boards will periodically take some time after a board meeting to discuss how the meeting went and what they might do differently.

Tenure Limits and Retirement Age

A traditional method of dealing with performance problems has been to set retirement limits. These limits are invariably used as an indirect and eventual way of getting directors who are not contributing off boards. Obviously this is not a very swift way to remedy performance issues. That's why we prefer an evaluation process.

However, we do believe that retirement age is important. Boards are notoriously slow to ease long-serving directors out of their ranks, even when their performance has long since ceased to be stellar. "We just don't want to hurt dear old Bill. He's seventy-one and retired as a CEO nine years ago. He's almost an institution. In his thirteen years here he has outlasted two other CEOs. It's true his performance has dimmed, but it isn't bad enough to ask him to leave." Dear old Bill indeed, but it's clear that another director would be more effective.

A clear retirement policy assures the board that such problems will be dealt with, and there is a growing consensus that directors should retire at around age seventy. We can't defend that number any more than we could defend sixty-five or seventy-five—in the end any retirement age is arbitrary. There are exceptional directors who energetically and productively contribute to their boards until they are well into their seventies, but for every one of these there are many more who are simply deadwood at much younger ages. Many directors in their seventies are slipping behind their colleagues. Their executive careers are ten or even fifteen years behind them; their networks have dwindled; and their business experience is becoming seriously dated. In a fast-changing business world, when more and more is being demanded of boards, these factors seriously hamper their effectiveness.

Another problem with keeping directors on boards after a certain age is that they occupy a place that could be filled by a younger person. In our view, many boards do need younger members who are more attuned to emerging consumer trends and developing technologies.

Another possibility for boards to consider is "term limits," which restrict directors from serving more than a certain number of terms. For example, directors who are elected for three-year terms might be limited to three or four such terms. There are some important advocates for reduced terms; for example, the Higgs Report in the United Kingdom suggested that non-executive directors should normally serve two three-year terms and only longer in exceptional circumstances.[9]

There are three caveats we have about such limits. The first is that it takes new independent directors a long time to learn about their company. Having term limits that are too short can remove them from the board too soon after they have gotten up to speed. Remember that most directors only spend between two to four weeks of work each year on their company—which will mean that after six years they will only have spent between twelve and twenty-four weeks on the job!

The second concern we have is that term limits can be used as an excuse for not conducting meaningful performance evaluations of individual directors. The excuse is, "We don't need to worry about Bill's poor contribution because he'll be gone at the end of his term." And third, directors can be forced to retire while they are still making a major contribution, which makes no sense.

There are many directors who have been on the same board for ten years or more, are still in their late fifties or early sixties, and still have "fire in the belly" for their task. CEOs and other directors tell us that this is often the case, and we have seen many examples ourselves. There is a case for retaining directors like these and not having term limits, but the price for doing so must be serious performance appraisal. What's more, the performance requirement might rise as tenure increases, particularly after the third term. By way of example, the CEO of one global professional services firm is elected by his fellow partners for a three-year term. The individual can proceed to a second or even a third term, but only if an increasing proportion of the firm's partners support reelection at each point. In the same spirit, we believe that a director seeking renomination for third or subsequent terms should have to do more than demonstrate that he doesn't constitute a serious problem.

Since the judicious injection of new blood strengthens board performance, it should be up to the board (through its corporate governance committee) to demonstrate that an incumbent's continued presence is a better option than a new director. The way that most boards work now, the long-serving incumbent has all the advantages, and it's too difficult to introduce a fresh face. With effective performance appraisal and "soft" term limits—the expectation that most directors will serve no more than nine or ten years, but that an exception can be made for extraordinary contributors—the situation can be reversed.

A final point on this matter. If there has been no movement on or off the board for several years, and if there is no prospect of change, we believe that in general, it would be appropriate to ask someone to leave to make room for a new director. Boards need to be refreshed with new ideas from new blood on a regular basis. An unchanging board, its members growing old together, will become less and less effective. So regardless of retirement age or tenure limits, change should be engineered if board membership has been static for too many years.

Refresh the Directors

D IRECTORS are elected to use the knowledge and wisdom accumulated over successful careers, and the unspoken assumption is that they already know most of what they need to know. But it's easy for them to slip into a routine. The board book arrives and is read. The meetings run to a schedule and each lasts for about the same time. The chances are that each director even occupies the same chair at the board table at every meeting. In such a climate, even good people can get stale. And they certainly can't be expected to keep up with all of the changing events that are affecting their company all by themselves. Yet very few boards offer knowledge-building opportunities to their directors except for brief orientations for new directors. In today's fast-changing business world, this is a missed opportunity to boost board performance. (Educating independent directors, who join boards without being very familiar with the company or its industry, is a related challenge that we'll discuss more fully in chapter 7.)

Ask for Directors' Own Ideas Regarding
Their "Continuing Education"

One way to refresh a board is to ask each director, every year, to identify an appropriate training initiative to enhance his ability to contribute. The initiative could be voluntary, but should be agreed to in consultation with the chairman or the head of the governance committee—because within reason, it could also be a legitimate company expense. Examples might include:

- Attending a seminar on shareholder value techniques if the company is using these to evaluate the performance of its businesses or new capital proposals

- Technical support in computer and Internet skills, so that the director can receive board materials by e-mail and access relevant information bases

- Attending programs that explore the ramifications of new requirements for boards and their committees (e.g., the Sarbanes-Oxley Act in the United States)

- Travel support for events such as industry conferences and trade shows, to enable the director to maintain a valuable professional network and understand more about customers and competitors

- Support for a director to join the company's executives in visiting peer "best practice benchmark" companies

Schedule a "Field Trip" to Bring
Directors Closer to the Company

We also think every board should schedule a trip each year to see some aspects of the company's distant operations or its customer base. The learning opportunities from these trips are immense. Aside from the obvious opportunity to meet staff and customers, there are considerable intangible gains from spending time traveling with senior executives and fellow directors. The informal discussions, extending over long meals and a glass of wine, are likely to be of a different character from the hurried discussions directors typically have with management or each other.

Utilize the Orientation Format in Other Efforts to Educate Directors

Finally, although companies are increasingly instituting a formal orientation program for new directors, these often fall into disrepair because the arrival of new directors is episodic. A number of directors have told us that their initial introductions to the company were so valuable that they'd love the opportunity to continue to learn in this way. We think boards would be more effective if directors had sessions like these on an ongoing basis. They might take the form of each director spending a day or two each year talking to a range of executives in a particular division or business unit. This would be in addition to the trips by the entire board.

Good initial orientation and ongoing learning experiences will produce an understanding of the company that would otherwise take many years of board meetings to achieve. Greater access to a range of executives and visits to major operations and key customers will accelerate directors' ability to understand the drivers of business performance as well as the caliber of the executive group—and these are critical bases for effective contribution.

Be Sensible About Director Compensation

IS BOARD COMPENSATION an important factor in assembling an effective board? Some see it as central to attracting good board candidates. Others talk about its influence on the way directors carry out their tasks. If the space given to it in directors' magazines and journals is any guide, it must be important. In fact, we disagree with much that is written about the subject, and believe its importance is exaggerated.

Let's start with the essential issues. The conventional wisdom is that every board must make two important decisions on compensation—how much and in what form. The first is rarely discussed in the literature; most boards simply find out what others pay through compensation surveys provided by consultants and follow suit. The second has been the subject of energetic debate. Remember our discussion in chapter 3 about the importance of aligning directors with shareholders' interests? The assumption seems to be that directors are motivated by money, so that putting their compensation at risk is the best way to ensure that they act effectively. Further, if they are paid in stock or options, they will focus on shareholder value. What do we make of this?

How Much?

There isn't a simple right or wrong answer to the question of how much someone should be paid in any profession. What they earn is a reflection of many factors, including market rates, the profitability of the business, and the contribution they make. We shouldn't expect pat answers for directors, either. Further, board compensation has its own special peculiarities. Directors on the same board are all paid the same, regardless of their performance and contribution. And reputation means nothing when it comes to the dollars. If a CEO such as Jack Welch accepts a seat on your board, he'll receive the same compensation as everyone else. Furthermore, directors of large companies often spend less time on the job than their peers on small company boards, but they are almost always paid more. In some industries, like software producers in the United States, directors are generally paid more than in other industries, with no evidence of more effort. Similarly, boards in different countries are paid differently. It's difficult to find a convincing logic for these practices—which means that we shouldn't be too surprised if the whole subject is more mystery than science.

Since boards generally resolve the issue of their compensation by engaging consultants to see what other companies pay, as with CEO compensation, we find the same result. Board compensation levels keep going up, simply because all boards seem to feel they should be in the upper half of such surveys. Differences in the amount of time the directors of different companies must devote to board business are ignored. Certainly, the performance of the board is not taken into account, and the legal and reputation risks a director assumes are rarely considered either. It all depends upon the survey!

Without any basis for determining what is reasonable compensation other than surveys, directors are vulnerable to accusations of greed. The legitimacy of boards—given their primary task to protect the interests of others—will be threatened if the prevailing community view is that directors have their noses in the trough. There is a real risk here. Many believe that boards have lost control of executive compensation, and it is only a short step from there to a view that board compensation is similarly out of control.[10]

It is therefore critically important for boards to ensure that the level of their compensation is justified. However, what's reasonable and what's greedy is largely a matter of opinion and is strongly influenced by the part of the world in which the board is at work. But boards can do better than simply following a survey of similar companies. Each board needs to establish a framework for deciding how much its members should be paid based on their own assessment of the task.

A sensible discussion about directors' pay can only take place after the board has discussed its role. The level of compensation should reflect the time that directors have to commit to their board duties. It might also reflect the extent to which the board is engaged in value-adding activities such as enhancing business strategy and delivering valued networks to the firm, as opposed to concentrating on a watch-dog role. It is harder to justify premium levels of compensation if the board contributes little to the growth of the business or if the directors carry out a very limited role.

One board discussed this issue and agreed that the directors should be seen as self-employed professionals who are, in essence, operating their "one person" professional firms. The question posed by this board was: What is a reasonable rate of pay for these people? The first step was to calculate the daily rate at which the board members were effectively being paid—the annual fees divided by an estimate of the number of days on the job. This was then compared to the rates that a professional adviser or consultant might charge, and it was on that basis that an assessment was made about whether the level of payment was reasonable. The Higgs Report makes a similar suggestion: that the level of remuneration of a non-executive director should be benchmarked against the daily remuneration of a senior representative of the company's professional advisers.[11]

As an example, and using research by consultancy William M. Mercer, the average annual remuneration of a U.S. director in 2000 was around $110,000.[12] According to a different survey, the average U.S. director spent around one hundred hours each year on the job, or around one hundred and fifty hours per year if travel time is included.[13] If we assume that travel time is part of the job, this equates to an hourly rate of around $700 per hour or about $6,000 per day for the *average* director in the United States. Would this amount be seen as low, reasonable, or excessive for a high caliber adviser in the U.S. market? Obviously the answer is in the eye of the beholder, but our main point is that we do believe that directors must be able to justify their remuneration by some reference to efforts and rewards in a comparable market.

There is one final point on the amount of compensation. Director retirement schemes are being dropped like hot potatoes in the United States, and institutional opposition to them is growing in the United Kingdom and Australia. By 2002, according to various reports, only around 3 percent of U.S. S&P 500 boards were offering director retirement schemes, whereas ten years ago almost all companies had them.[14] These schemes are now seen as "perks" that accrue regardless of business performance. We don't argue with that view, although we tend to see them as simply another form of director remuneration, albeit one paid in a less transparent form. Retirement schemes can be a large but somewhat hidden proportion of directors' compensation. Dropping them, and if necessary increasing the compensation level, is a more transparent way to proceed.

How Should It Be Paid?

With regard to the currency to be used, so-called best practice is based more on fashionable dogma than empirical evidence. Only a few years ago, governance experts were telling us that directors should receive compensation in cash. This supposedly reduced the potential for conflict of interest. Directors paid this way would be more likely to act in the interests of both large and small shareholders in the short and the longer term. Best practice has come a full 180 degrees in the past five years—good governance requires directors to have serious skin in the game, with most of their remuneration at risk and in stock.

Consider these views of corporate governance experts in the United States:

> The risk can't be only on the investors, the institutions, and the little guys. The director has to share in that pain.[15]

> This is the way it is supposed to work. If stock prices go up, directors and shareholders feel great. If prices go down, they don't feel great, and directors have real incentive to make things go great again.[16]

The trends are clear—directors should own serious amounts of the company's stock; they should receive their compensation mostly in stock (and therefore have it at risk), and options are a good idea. These ideas are a reality in the United States, where more than half of total director pay is now in stock or options; nearly all companies pay at least part of their director remuneration in stock; and over half now offer options to directors.[17] These trends are being repeated around the world. There is still opposition to options for U.K. and Australian directors, but payment in stock is increasingly supported.

As we indicated in chapter 3, we are skeptical about the huge importance given to financial alignment in today's governance debate.

Our own experience is that directors' readiness to work hard and effectively is scarcely related to their level or type of compensation. We work with many boards and simply don't see the importance of this alignment in practice. In fact, we often see the same individuals earning very different levels and types of remuneration on different company boards. These directors' diligence and motivation appear to be quite independent of their compensation and how they receive it. As we said earlier, research supports this view. Directors report that compensation is not an important reason for serving on boards.[18] Instead, they say they serve on boards primarily to learn.

The literature tells us that incentive compensation should be tied to factors that can be controlled, and the quality and performance of the board is only one of many factors that might affect share price. The more recent executive compensation schemes acknowledge this, accepting that it is unwise to tie compensation directly to movements in the stock price. If such a tie is established, the rising tide of a bull market will enrich both executives and directors, regardless of whether they are hard working and wise or not.

There is another aspect to this question. If all or a large part of directors' remuneration is at risk and in equity, only wealthy people are likely to be able to serve on boards. Others may not be able to afford the initial investment or to forgo the cash income. If one seeks diversity of experience on boards, this could be a problem.

We aren't philosophically opposed to directors' options (as some jurisdictions are), but we believe that such incentives based on targets are management's territory, and that it's the board's job to design those incentives.[19] If directors have similar incentives they will soon—and not without reason—be accused of setting soft management targets to enrich themselves. On the other hand, we see no reason why directors shouldn't share in wealth that has already been created. To illustrate the principle we are trying to establish, we worked with one board to create an options scheme for directors, one that was quite different from the scheme offered to the management team.

Management had stretch targets—their options only were granted if company performance rated well against peer companies, and the option strike prices were also higher than the current price. For the directors, however, the options were simply a reward for the company's current performance. The directors' options, a modest number, were issued if the company met profit targets relative to peer companies. A director could exercise her options at the current price, but not until a year after she had left the board. In other words, if the stock price fell, the options had no value, so directors had every reason to leave the company in very good shape when they retired.

In summary, while we believe directors should own some shares, if for no other reason than appearance of that ownership, there is little to gain from the more extreme proposals. They trivialize directors' motivation by overemphasizing the importance of the money, make it impossible for some competent directors to serve, and make it hard for directors to be objective about management's pay schemes.

Our cautionary note about the use of stock to compensate directors is shared by the CEOs in our survey. While there are differences across countries, many CEOs, even in the United States, are unconvinced about requiring directors to own substantial amounts of stock and placing their compensation mostly at risk (table 6-1).

TABLE 6 - 1

CEOs Don't Support the "Financial Alignment" Argument

	PERCENT OF CEOs AGREEING WITH PROPOSITION, BY REGION		
Proposition	**North America**	**Europe**	**Asia Pacific**
Outside directors should be required to own stock in the business in amounts that are very material to them (C-5)	52	27	40
Remuneration of outside directors should substantially be at risk— being paid in stock and options (C-6)	41	17	34

Note: The CEOs responded to a 5 point scale where 1 = Strongly Disagree to 5 = Strongly Agree. We have classified 1 and 2 as "disagree" and 4 and 5 as "agree."

Source: BCG HBS Global Survey of 132 CEOs in 2001.

Following the Enron debacle—and the host of problems that followed in other companies—we may see a shift in the debate about directors' compensation because of fears that directors' concern with stock prices makes them more susceptible to inflated forecasts, creative accounting treatments, and manipulation. Some critics feel that the attitudes such schemes generated among U.S. CEOs carried over to boardrooms. Perhaps the wheel will come full circle and the old orthodoxy will reappear—namely, that cash retainers will ensure directors' best attention to their task. However, our view here, as in the other aspects of board design, is that directors should focus on solutions that fit their circumstances.

In this chapter we have described the design elements needed to attract and motivate a group of directors who have the right skills and knowledge. In chapter 7 we turn to the issues of information and its utilization. Without a clear grasp of its company's business model and its performance, no board can be effective.

CHAPTER seven

Building Knowledge
and Using It Wisely

"We get an enormous amount of information, but it is still hard to know what is really going on."   —DIRECTOR

"We keep on having to repeat things. They forget what we have told them in previous meetings."
                                    —SENIOR EXECUTIVE

"It seemed that the board was the last to know, and yet the industry 'dogs' had been barking for some time about the company."   —INVESTMENT ANALYST

BOARDS THAT ARE COMMITTED TO INCREASING THEIR useful knowledge about their companies—and we find many that already are—will find it helpful to explore changes in four areas, which we'll first describe in broad strokes, then tackle in greater detail in the remainder of the chapter. (You'll no doubt recognize underlying them some of the points we've been emphasizing through-out the book.) They are:

> *Using the directors' time more productively:* Too many board meet-ings are "show and tell" affairs rather than deep conversations with management and among the directors. And too much time in these meetings is devoted to relatively insignificant matters rather than to major strategic issues. Boards also tend to concentrate on the pres-ent and the recent past in their meetings, rather than on future challenges and opportunities. That's why board meetings, in gen-eral, need to be revamped from the ground up, both in terms of content and format. And why should directors' time be taken up solely in meetings in the first place? Too many directors never see what the business looks like from any other vantage point than their seats at the boardroom table. Too often, they are isolated from the rest of the company. They see it only through the information that management provides. They need to broaden their contacts inside and outside the organization so that they can call on a range of resources to enhance their understanding of the business.
>
> *Thinking more strategically about "information":* Most boards receive lots of information—or perhaps more accurately, they receive a lot of paper or e-mail—but it can be difficult to pick out what is really important. This is because most of the material they receive isn't particularly memorable or well organized, so it's not surprising that many directors forget much of it. What directors need is information that focuses on the important issues and ensures that they understand the real drivers of performance and the major elements of risk. Boards also need to take greater advan-tage of the latest computer technology to gain continual access to information. In the twenty-first century, they should not have to wait until they receive information from management; they should be able to seek and access much of it on their own, electronically.
>
> *Encouraging directors to focus:* For reasons we pointed out in chapter 3, directors see themselves as generalists, but in a world in which there is more to know than time to learn it, this puts them

at a serious disadvantage. They simply can't know all that needs to be understood. Faced with this difficulty, directors may more often have to divide up their work to get the job done well.

Designing effective processes for monitoring performance: While most boards have processes for dealing with traditional audit and compensation issues because of the committees established for those purposes, they also need well-designed processes for engaging in strategy development and assessment and top management appraisal and succession—activities that are central to their task. Effective boards must think deeply about how they engage in these activities, and be certain they develop the knowledge needed to accomplish them.

None of these ideas for improvement involve rocket science. The steps that boards need to take to build and use knowledge are relatively straightforward. Yet, because boards are always so busy, they rarely stop to look at why they are struggling and to consider solutions that may be readily available to them.

Making the Most of Limited Time

As we have been emphasizing, directors, especially those who are non-executives, are part-timers. Yet it takes time to understand their company and to use this knowledge. Here are a few thoughts on how to address this dilemma.

Get More Value from Board Meetings

The time that the board spends together in meetings is arguably the most important time that directors devote to their duties. It is in board meetings that the whole board is engaged, that ideas are contested, and that the board develops a collective view, which it then conveys to management. The board meeting is truly the place and time when directors learn most about their company and when they make decisions. The first order of business, then, is thinking through how often the board should meet, how long each meeting should last, and what should be on the agenda.

There are many mysteries about why boards do what they do, and nowhere is this more evident than when we try to make sense of the frequency and length of their meetings. Practice varies a great deal around the world, and the differences seem unrelated to the complexity of the businesses. Instead, national traditions and company habit seem to explain the variety in practice. Boards in the United Kingdom and Australia have traditionally met almost monthly. U.S. boards have met less frequently, currently averaging around seven times per year, but there is an enormous spread of practice even within the same industry.[1] German supervisory boards meet on average five times per year, Swiss and French boards average around six, Dutch and Swedish boards average around eight, while Italian boards meet ten times each year.[2] Traditionally, in most of these places, the board meetings have been quite brief, frequently little more than half a day each time.

Today, there are some signs of a global convergence around eight meetings per year. Spencer Stuart's 2002 survey places the U.S. board average at seven and a half meetings, while Heidrick & Struggles' 2003 European survey confirms eight meetings.[3] In other words, eight regular meetings is now the average on both sides of the Atlantic. Australian boards, which have historically met most frequently, are also starting to wind back from their monthly meetings, with some of the largest companies settling on between seven and nine meetings each year.[4] Statistically, at least, there is some convergence going on, so it is a good time to ask whether this outcome makes sense.

While such averages are interesting, they can actually mask the really important question: What is the right number—and length—of meetings? This depends on the size and complexity of the company and the directors' definition of their role. As we discussed in chapter 4, boards can take a legitimately different view of what their role should be. Some will be watchdogs and delegate more to management, while others, for a variety of reasons, will want to be more involved. And even with a similar role, a more complex company or one that is in trouble will demand more of the directors' time.

While we should expect to see significant differences in practice between boards—hopefully based on careful consideration of their role rather than blind adherence to tradition—there are some generalizations that give us a good starting point. Monthly meetings, in our experience, can encourage boards to slip into a routine focused on detailed monthly results that is rarely meaningful. Also, they can be a huge imposition on executive and director time. On the other hand, the practice of boards overseeing hugely complex companies in just four or five half-day meetings each year seems clearly inadequate. How can a director in anything but the simplest company understand what is happening in such a limited time? For most companies, somewhere between six and nine meetings are necessary to enable directors to stay in touch with each other and their company. Thus the growing convergence around eight meetings per year may be sensible. Of course, other special meetings in person or by telephone can be added to cope with unusual situations such as a major acquisition or the illness of the CEO. And more and more boards are finding it useful to have one multiday (usually two-day) meeting a year, often to discuss strategic issues in depth.

We should emphasize it's not just the number of meetings that concerns us. Too often we find that, having gotten all the directors together, too little time is scheduled at each meeting. Again the schedule is the result of tradition rather than careful planning. Adding meetings is hard to do because it often requires extra travel or more frequent interruptions in directors' other activities. It is obviously easier, given the busy schedules of the directors, to extend the board meetings by a few hours rather than scheduling an extra meeting. An hour or two may not seem like much, but think about it—an hour added to what has been a four- or five-hour meeting gives the board 20 to 25 percent more time together. This is not an inconsequential increment.

For most companies, somewhere between six and nine full-day meetings will be required. Some of the larger and more complex companies will find that each meeting, including time allocated for committees to meet, extends into a second day. Boards are beginning to experiment with different schedules. One bank, with operations spread across several continents, has moved from twelve to eight meetings each year, but each lasts for nearly two days. The first half-day is spent on board committee work, and then the board meeting occupies the afternoon and the morning of the following day. There is always a presentation scheduled on some aspect of the bank's business that is designed not for any decisions to be made but rather to allow directors to learn more about a complicated aspect of the business. There is also usually a dinner in the evening where the guests might include staff, clients, or other industry participants.

Whatever the meeting schedule, the next important issue concerns the meeting agenda. As we said earlier, directors frequently tell us that they spend too little time discussing strategic issues. We will come shortly to the question of how boards should become involved in the strategy process, but what typically happens is that the agenda is dominated by reviewing what has recently happened, routine items, and urgent issues that need approval. As a result, directors strongly complain that they don't have enough opportunities to think beyond the present and the recent past.

One simple way to deal with this concern is to reserve at least half of every board meeting to focus on two things:

- Major issues affecting the company's future
- Discussions (not just presentations) with key executives about the issues facing the company's major business(es)

To identify such major issues, the CEO and the board at the start of each year should agree on the five to ten key issues that are likely to be at the heart of the company's success over the next five to ten years. For boards that hold them, most of these issues will emerge from the annual strategy retreat. These should then be scheduled in the board calendar for discussion throughout the following year. Management might prepare discussion papers to be read by the directors in advance so adequate time can be allocated at board meetings for discussions. Typically, these will be important issues that might not otherwise make the board agendas because there is no crisis that directs the board's attention to them. They might include topics like the sources of future growth, how the company is doing in developing talent, postacquisition reviews, analysis of competitor strategies, the state of product development, the future shape of the business portfolio, or the strength of the company's brands.

Unless a board has concluded that it's not its role to delve into individual business units, meeting agendas must make room for unrushed discussion about each of the major businesses. In most boards, the time set aside for businesses without problems is all too often cut short because the board meeting runs late or the time allocated to the meeting itself is too short.

When this happens, senior executives who have been asked to discuss their business are kept waiting outside the boardroom, and then are told they have twenty rather than the originally scheduled forty minutes to talk about an issue that is vital to them. They know they can't run over time, because some of the directors have planes to catch, so they're forced to slice and dice the material they were hoping to present for consideration. This prevents thoughtful discussion and good decision making on critical issues, and tends to undercut the motivation of the managers affected. It's also insulting to them. In our experience, such problems usually occur because the chairman and whoever is helping him with the agenda planning try to cram too much into the time available.

While we're on this point, we should mention that we feel strongly that when an executive is asked to talk about his business, he should be given *an hour or more,* not just thirty minutes. A serious defect in most boards is that there are too few informal and informed discussions with management other than the CEO. If directors are to truly understand their company, they must spend quality time talking about the major issues with the executives directly involved.

One good approach is to schedule major business reviews on a rolling basis so that at least once annually each senior executive gets meaningful time in discussion with the board. Again, to save meeting time, the board should read the presentation material beforehand, and only the first few minutes should be spent answering any questions of clarification. Then—and this happens extraordinarily rarely today—the board can spend an hour or more discussing the business with the senior executives responsible for it. The directors will be learning from this interaction, and the executives will benefit from the directors' advice.

We would like to see less time taken with the ubiquitous Power-Point presentations, carefully rehearsed by the executive group, because we feel such show and tell sessions don't allow for the board to really engage in a discussion, nor do they permit the board to assess the caliber of the executive running the business. "Death by PowerPoint" is how one non-executive director described his board's meetings to us. What most boards badly need is more informal discussion with key executives and among themselves. From our work with boards it is clear that such discussions—question-and-answer sessions as well as mutual exploration of issues—rarely take place. As more than one director has told us, "We spend so much time listening politely to management presentations that there is no time to discuss strategic issues."

Smart agenda planners schedule important topics at the beginning of the meeting to make sure they are given adequate time. If time is tight at the end of the meeting, the items "squeezed" are generally the less-crucial routine reports. It's a good idea, though, to vary the sequence, so that the same items don't get short shrift repeatedly. Some boards obtain more discussion time by dividing meetings into two distinct halves. The first part includes presentations about performance or requiring specific board action, and the second half is spent in less-formal discussions with management about the important but less-pressing topics. The advantage of this approach is that it preserves scarce time for deep discussions between the board and management. Nothing is permitted to interfere with this interaction.

Move Directors Outside the Boardroom

We think about 90 percent of most directors' time is spent either alone reading board reports, with their colleagues around the board table, or having occasional conversations with small groups of directors. For most directors, hardly any time is spent in conversation with down-the-line managers, visiting plants or key customers, or talking to industry experts about competitors or overseas trends.

Yet it's also true that almost every time a company fails or stumbles, industry experts saw the fall coming before the board. The board is often the last to know that its company has serious problems. That's why we feel strongly that directors should have regular contact with managers, and schedule less-regular (at least occasional) meetings with industry analysts and other experts. (Many directors tell us that they learn more about the business in casual conversation with management—often during meals or while traveling to company facilities—than they do in board meetings.) While directors should treat *external* views—from industry experts—with caution, it's a mistake not to know what's being said in the industry. Even inviting them to board meetings occasionally to listen to their ideas can be a good idea.

There is one ground rule that directors should usually follow in talking to management. Most CEOs want to know when such conversations are taking place, and this is not unreasonable. Such contacts should not undermine the CEO's relationship with subordinates. With that caveat, we are convinced that it is productive for directors to discuss business issues with senior executives on management's own turf rather than just in the boardroom. The CEOs in our survey do not completely agree with us and are ambivalent about directors moving outside the boardroom (see appendix, Proposition C-3). They are almost equally divided between those who believe directors should spend more time talking to employees, customers, and suppliers, those who do not, and those who are unsure. This is not surprising, since CEOs may feel that directors nosing around operations or visiting customers can be a complication to their already busy lives. Nevertheless, we believe it is important, and can be done in a way that does not undermine the CEO's leadership.

One way such visits can begin is with the orientation of new directors. As mentioned in chapter 6, some boards have decided that these meetings are so valuable to new directors that they want to extend them for all board members periodically. In fact, many directors also report that an occasional trip to distant operations, accompanying the senior executive group, can transform relationships with senior management, allow them to meet local staff, as well as build knowledge. While such trips can be criticized as a "boondoggle," we believe that they can be an immense help to directors, well worth the time and expense.

Keep in mind that our objective is not to eliminate—or even minimize—the CEO as a major source of the board's information. Boards are dependent on their CEO for information for good reason. Instead, we want to expand the directors' sources of information so they can have a broader view of their company and improve their ability to offer advice, make decisions, and monitor their company's progress.

A More Strategic Approach to Information

EVEN IN BOARDS that adopt these practices, most of the knowledge directors use in their deliberations is based on information received from management, but the state of such information is problematic. Most directors tell us they are overwhelmed with the *volume* of material they receive but "underwhelmed" by the *content*. No wonder directors forget much of what they have read between meetings and frustrate executives by asking them to repeat it. To solve this problem, directors (along with management) must more carefully define the information the board needs and must figure out ways to make it more memorable. New technology makes this much easier to accomplish.

Identify the Information Needed

We cannot define in detail the specific information a particular board should receive—that can only be done on a company-by-company basis. Nor can we describe the format in which information should be presented, important as that is. A simple graph, for example, can be much more informative than a whole page of numbers. What we can do here is encourage directors to think about the sort of information they need and how it can best be organized in relation to what they want to know. For example, imagine a director who has been on a board for three years. Shouldn't she have the information to answer questions like these:

1. Where is shareholder value being created and destroyed in our company? Do we know which businesses earn in excess of the cost of capital?

2. What are the long-term (three to five years) margin trends in our businesses?

3. What are the major risks to which the company is exposed, and are these being managed effectively?

4. Are there any financial reporting issues in which our accounting practices would be regarded as "aggressive"?

5. What major projects are under way in the company (capital projects as well as "change" projects), and is implementation on schedule and on cost?

6. What is the level of employee morale? What is the retention rate for our key people? Do we survey employees' attitudes and, if so, what do they say? How are we doing in developing and retaining talent?

7. Is our market share in key segments holding? What are the trends in customer satisfaction?

8. What is happening to our major brands and our corporate image? Are these getting stronger or being eroded?

9. How does our strategy differ from that of our competitors in our major businesses?

10. How is our stock viewed by the analysts who cover us? Are we a "buy, hold, or sell" for brokers? On what do they base their view?

Too many directors seem to drown in numbers but can't answer even very basic questions like these. If board members were to score themselves against this list—and we encourage each board to "design" its own list—they would likely identify important gaps in their knowledge about the company. If they score highly, they can be confident that they are well prepared to carry out their role, however defined.

We are not suggesting that all the information needed to answer questions like these is to be provided on a monthly or even quarterly basis. Information will best be converted to real knowledge if it's provided when it is needed to understand specific issues. What boards must do is periodically take stock and ask themselves a broad set of questions like these. If they feel underinformed, they must work with management to determine how and when the answers will be provided.

Make Information More Memorable

Even when directors are getting the information they feel they need, many of them have problems retaining their knowledge from one meeting to the next. It's such an embarrassing problem that it is likely to be discreetly swept under the carpet. Yet this problem has been raised in almost every board review we have performed, in part reflecting the frustration felt by executives who believe that directors should do better to remember what they have been told or have read. While most CEOs in our survey feel that this is not a problem, more than 40 percent of them—a sizable minority—are unsure, or believe directors don't retain information they have been given at prior meetings (see appendix, Proposition B-3). How comfortable is it leading a discussion when you wonder whether your directors retained information they were given before?

We believe that most of the directors who forget things do so not because they are lazy or incompetent but because it's very difficult not to. The amount of information they need to master is growing rapidly. Markets are changing at an ever-increasing rate. The task of remembering—let alone keeping up with change—is formidable for part-time directors who immediately have to turn their minds to other matters when board meetings are over, and who are often faced with gaps of two months between meetings.

To make information more memorable, directors need frameworks to help them capture and hold on to the crucial elements in the flood of information that comes their way. If they do not have a *model* of the business in their minds, they will struggle to absorb more than a small fraction of the data they get. Most directors receive the traditional financial statements, and separately they will receive a small mountain of information about volumes produced and sold in each business or territory, and the costs associated with these. It really helps if models can be developed that integrate all these numbers so that it is possible to see more clearly those key factors that drive financial outcomes.

There are tools available that can help in this task, for example, the *Balanced Scorecard*.[5] The objective in such efforts is to show how high-level company goals can be systematically tied to specific activities that are carried out deep in the company. Such an understanding guides the director to the important leverage points.

Such models are needed to help directors cope with complexity, and to ensure that they focus on the things that really matter. Our proposition is that directors struggle to retain information not only because they are busy part timers but also because they haven't developed good "models of the business" to illuminate the way it works. Strange to say, but they often don't have a robust understanding of how money is made. They don't know the leverage points and what really drives profitability. In this situation they will continue to struggle to absorb the information thrown at them.

It follows that an important task for management—particularly the chief financial officer—and the board is to figure out ways to explain and describe how the business model really works. What are the key drivers of success for the company and/or its component parts? When they understand these well, directors will be able to make better use of the information available to them.

Take Advantage of the New Accessibility

New technology can help in this task as well, and a number of boards are beginning to provide their members rapid access to information. For example, the Australian telephone company, Telstra, has an information system online for its directors. It includes agendas, minutes, and information for both the board and committees (current and past since the system was introduced), board and audit committee charters, policies, announcements by the company to the stock exchange, news clippings, news summaries, and a few other matters. It also includes a secure e-mail system for communication with directors.

A few companies, ahead of the field, are developing intranet-based systems that enable boards to have relevant performance information at their fingertips. Information from a multitude of reports can be reorganized, summarized, and added to a database, and "easy to use" graphical information can be accessed by the directors. They can, if they wish, "drill down" to get more detail and explore the underlying causalities in the numbers.

These developments offer directors unprecedented freedom to peruse company data that until now was only available if they asked for it—and if management spent a lot of time compiling and organizing it. There are advantages of these systems for management, because requests for information from directors can be onerous. On the other hand, some CEOs will worry about directors wandering around in management databases. Yet we believe that directors have an obligation to explore data to develop their understanding, and that they must insist that management makes it available. In the final analysis, though, the effective use of such data will depend on the directors' understanding of their company's underlying business model. Without this, more and rapid data access is likely to lead only to more confusion.

Encouraging Directors to Adopt a Focus

Focus is central to any discussion about knowledge "productivity." And make no mistake; encouraging directors to adopt a focus requires no less than a major paradigm shift in the way that boards conceive of how their members should work together.

At issue is how directors *manage knowledge*. There is universal agreement that the core board committees allow a subset of the directors to focus on and learn about audit and compensation matters (and now governance issues) in great depth. The existence of these committees acknowledges the magnitude of the part-time director's task, and the need for focus. However, that is where the specialization ends on most boards.

We believe this is a missed opportunity. As we argued earlier, boards are "knowledge organizations," and for such groups, the effective response to complexity is to specialize and focus. In that spirit, we believe that each director should be encouraged to build deeper knowledge in a couple of areas that are important to the board's performance. They should be encouraged to take a topic or issue and focus on it in greater depth. The objective is not only to be better informed, but also to be a better contributor to the discussions among all board members. This deeper focus is not to be confused with executive responsibility. That remains management's prerogative.

Some boards are experimenting in this direction. Several years ago, one bank we know well allocated seven topics, for example executive development, among its outside directors, and asked each director to "go a little more deeply" into one of those topics. Surprisingly, it was the CEO who proposed this arrangement in the face of board misgivings about "becoming too involved." So far, the verdict of both CEO and board is positive. The directors believe they are more knowledgeable, and the CEO agrees and also does not feel the directors are interfering with management.

In general, we do not support the allocation of specific businesses or functions to individual directors, because that would directly duplicate management accountabilities—which could cause tension between managers and directors. Rather, we prefer that directors focus on topics that ideally cut across the portfolio—for example, the use of technology, executive development, or investment in Asia. The assignments should also have sunset clauses of a year or two to make sure they don't become too institutionalized. Each director's task would be to go out of his way to become more informed about one such subject. For example, if major investment in Asia is a key issue across the portfolio, the designated director (or even two) might seek to understand which other companies are investing there and with what success. She would build networks of experienced contacts, perhaps receive geographic publications, talk occasionally to consultants and others involved in the region, and so forth. She might occasionally meet with peers—such as directors of other companies—who are engaged in the region. She would also make sure she understood the views of the company's own key executives. Similarly, if executive development is the topic because of its importance to the company, our director might join company executives when they visit other best practice firms. He might also spend time visiting the company's internal executive education programs, and he would certainly spend time talking to executives about their experience in such programs, and their perspectives on their careers.

We encourage boards to experiment with this way of increasing the board's capacity to deal with a wide variety of complex business issues. Our primary intention is to enhance knowledge at the board level so that directors can be well informed and even genuinely insightful in their deliberations. But there is an additional and substantial benefit— directors will learn more about the company as a whole, even as they explore a narrow slice of it.

They will learn more *because they will have a reason to be proactive.* The role of most non-executive directors can be very reactive and passive, which seriously limits their incentive and capacity to learn. Their task today is to read and comment on material that has been wholly prepared by other people, usually management. Expecting them to be more focused will help them to *engage.*

Again it goes without saying that certain protocols should be observed when on "assignment." Directors obviously need to understand that their purpose is to learn on behalf of their fellow directors, and not to interfere with management. They also need to understand and accept that their responsibility is to inform their board colleagues including the CEO about what they have learned.

As we point out in chapter 3, some directors may be uncomfortable about the increased accountability or even the additional work inherent in this approach. Some CEOs may fear it as an intrusion onto management's patch. Other directors may argue that a board's responsibilities as well as its accountability should be shared among all the directors. They argue, therefore, that it is inappropriate to put individual directors in the position where they are regarded as the expert to whom the board defers. This is an objection we frequently encounter, but it is hard to reconcile with another widely held view—that it is appropriate to search for new directors to bring special skills onto the board. In conventional board wisdom, it seems appropriate to bring new expertise onto the board, but not to develop and utilize these skills after directors are elected!

While directors still seem committed to their generalist stance, we believe that greater focus is key to governance excellence in complex businesses. The majority of the CEOs we surveyed agree that to deal with complexity, directors will have to allocate some issues among themselves (see appendix, Proposition C-2).

Knowledge management has been a hot topic for executives in recent years, and for very good reason. But it is a subject that boards now need to consider. Our proposals give boards the opportunity to experiment with new forms of knowledge management. Many directors are concerned about their capacity to keep up with fast-moving business developments, and these pressures are likely to increase. If directors cannot spend much more time on each board, greater focus is the most sensible response.

Using Knowledge: Two Key Processes

THERE IS a funny thing about knowledge. The more you use it, the more you understand it. Further, the more directors share knowledge among themselves, the more they all know. The strategy development and CEO performance appraisal processes are two key board activities in which directors' develop, use, and share their understanding. These two processes build the knowledge that boards need even as they do their job. The first gives directors insight into the health and direction of the company and its businesses. The second informs them about management and how well the board as a whole believes the CEO is doing his job. It identifies issues where there is a consensus that things are going well and not so well, in addition to areas of disagreement among directors.

The aspiration of every board we have worked with is to "spend more time on strategy." Directors are frustrated because they don't have enough time to devote to these issues. One challenge facing boards is to come to grips with how strategy is actually developed inside their company, because the board process cannot be designed independently of that.

Any multibusiness company (and most companies do have more than one business) will periodically agonize over the appropriate relationship between their corporate center and the individual businesses. Is it "hands off" or directive? Is the head office role more akin to that of a financial holding company, or is it very much engaged in defining each business strategy? Is the planning process mostly "top down" or "bottom up"?

A board cannot define how it is to be involved in developing strategy independent of how management thinks about these matters. It would not work, for example, for the board to want to talk to the business heads early in the planning cycle if this is inconsistent with the way the CEO wants the planning process to work. This point seems so obvious, yet it is never raised as an issue in the discussion on boards. Boards are routinely urged to get involved in strategy, but it is advice that is unencumbered by any practical appreciation of how this might be done and the obstacles to doing so. The result can be frustration on the part of directors and managers.

Our advice to boards seeking a meaningful engagement in strategy development is to start by addressing the following issues:

- First, the board must define the scope of its strategic involvement by relating it to its chosen role. Does it want to be only a watchdog or is it seeking more active involvement? Is the board interested primarily in "corporate" strategy—financial goals and the shape of the portfolio, or does it want to be seriously involved in the development of strategies in *each* or some of the major businesses? Whatever choice is made, the board must have the information and knowledge needed.

- Second, does the board want to be involved at the start of management's planning process and occasionally during it—or is it content to review the plan when management has largely completed it? The more involved the directors expect to be in shaping strategy, the earlier they need to start talking with management and among themselves.

- Third, the board must clarify whether its expectations for engagement are congruent with the philosophy of the executives who are leading the corporation, especially the CEO. It cannot be more interventionist in individual businesses than corporate management, and it cannot act earlier in the planning process than they do. It can't be "top down" if the corporate center is mostly "bottom up." If, for example, the board wants to offer comment and critique as business plans are developed, its aspirations must be reconciled with the management process rather than be pursued independently.

- Finally, boards need to understand that developing strategy is a repetitive process, rather like taking layers off the onion. Annual strategy retreats, where the board and senior executives go away for two or three days to talk about the main issues facing the company are mostly well received because they enable deeper discussions to take place among directors and between them and management. Yet we offer a caution, because these retreats can be based on a flawed assumption that strategic planning is a one-shot affair. It isn't. Instead, the process requires continual board involvement, as the board at Delphi, described in chapter 1, clearly recognized. The strategic issues addressed in an annual retreat early in the year must be picked up throughout the remainder of the year and progressively discussed until sufficient clarity is achieved. Unless this is recognized, directors will become frustrated, because their experience will be seen as superficial. What happens in effective boards is that the

strategy retreat opens up discussion about a number of issues
that are progressively dealt with at subsequent board meetings
over the ensuing year.

Another key process in which boards need to be involved is the
evaluation of their CEO. It obviously is a key to effective monitoring of
company performance and is also a way for directors to build their
understanding of how they all see their company and its leader.

Too often we have seen boards give lip service to the fact that
they are doing such an evaluation. However, with a little probing, what
we find is that the compensation committee members, as they work
through the formula for determining the CEO's compensation, have a
conversation among themselves about his performance. This is almost
always too superficial, and really misses the point, because the whole
board is not involved.

What we have in mind is much more thorough, and should involve
all the independent board members, and maybe even management
directors and other senior executives as well. Each board should design
a process that fits its circumstances—including especially its relationship with its CEO. However, we believe that an effective process
should touch these bases:

- It should allow the CEO to provide the board with her assessment of her performance for the past year, as well as the non-
  quantitative goals she sets for herself for the next year, for
  example, to work on developing candidates as her successor, to
  make a major acquisition, or to improve the company's performance in the European region.

- It should enable directors to make the distinction between "performance" by the CEO and the "results" achieved by the company. Obviously the financial and competitive results the
  company achieves must be considered in the evaluation. However, many times CEOs perform very effectively even as their
  company is going through a bad period competitively or in terms
  of its financial results. Effective evaluation must allow directors
  to make this distinction and to evaluate their CEO accordingly.

- It should allow the directors to make their own individual assessments of their CEO. This can be done in many formats— a written questionnaire; by asking each director to write a memorandum describing his thoughts; or by having each director interviewed, for example, by a member of the corporate governance or compensation committee.

- These individual assessments should be summarized on an anonymous basis. This can be done by the board chairman, if he's not the CEO, by the lead director, or by a committee chairman.

- This consensus view should be shared with all the independent directors, and there should be a discussion among them before a final version of the evaluation is reached.

- More than one director (again the board chairman, if not the CEO, or the lead director and/or a committee chairman) should meet with the CEO and discuss the evaluation with her.

The reasons for most of these steps are probably self-evident, but we do want to stress a few of them. For example, we like to see a discussion among all the directors not only because it is their responsibility, but also because it's a great learning opportunity. Such discussion will help them understand how other board members see the CEO's performance, and also the state of the company. As a result they will develop a more robust, shared perspective, which is critical to board effectiveness.

We suggest that more than one director be involved in providing feedback to the CEO so that the communication is valid. Performance feedback is an emotional process. Too often both the person delivering the appraisal and the one receiving it can become defensive and mishear what is intended; this applies to CEOs and directors like everyone else. Having more than one director involved assures a more accurate communication process.

The issue of whether to also include management directors and other senior executives in this activity is a bit complex. On the negative side, they are the CEO's subordinates, and this could make the insiders' involvement complicated and inhibiting to the outside directors.

On the other hand, it is very important that the outside directors have a good understanding of the leadership style and skills of the CEO as well as whether he is respected by the executive team. Of course, there are many companies today that use 360-degree evaluations, and their bosses are likely to be quite accustomed to getting feedback from those who work for them. Whatever its source, boards must have an accurate view of how their CEO is perceived from within.

However it is done—and we urge boards to design their own processes along the lines we have described—the CEO evaluation is a key opportunity for directors to build and use their knowledge. It will cause them to reflect on their own understanding. It will enable them to learn how other directors feel. Finally, it will enable them to understand how their CEO feels about his progress as well as that of the company.

These two processes are only two of the many steps we have described that boards can take to build the knowledge in the limited time individual directors have available. As we have stressed throughout, each board must design its structure, membership, and processes to fit its chosen role.

A test of how well any design fits the board's circumstances is whether it enables them to know their company and build on that knowledge. Directors are continually challenged by the difficulties of learning about their company in the limited time available. That problem is not going to go away, so boards must take every opportunity to rethink and challenge the ways in which they currently learn about the business. Board processes and activities easily acquire a life of their own and continue as if on "autopilot" for many years. Good boards will periodically revisit these activities to ask whether they are adding value—which generally will mean, "Are they helping us to better understand the important issues facing this company?" If they aren't helping, it likely is time to return to the drawing board again.

eight

Behind Closed Doors

*"I feel that I can only ask two or three tough questions be-
fore I start to feel that I am being a nuisance."*
— NON-EXECUTIVE DIRECTOR

*"I will disagree with a director, but I'm always very careful
about how I do it, and I only do it if asked my opinion."*
— SENIOR EXECUTIVE

MOST OF THE WORK DONE BY A BOARD TAKES PLACE
in the privacy of the boardroom. That is where directors
discuss matters among themselves and with management, offer advice,
assess proposals, and make decisions. Rarely, if ever, does any information on how the members contribute as individuals or work together as
a group escape to the world outside.

The same is true about the more limited interactions among board
members and with managers outside of the boardroom. E-mails, phone
calls, committee meetings—all are exclusive to the participants. It's
almost impossible for anyone "outside the circle" to get an accurate

reading on whether pressing issues are receiving the appropriate scrutiny with pertinent information at hand, and whether decisions are being made with due consideration and thorough discussion—in sum, whether the board is performing to its potential. That the work of boards takes place "behind closed doors" is the major reason we are skeptical about many of the current proposals for board reform.

Take, for example, a 2002 recommendation of the New York Stock Exchange: that the name of the director who presided over meetings of the independent directors be disclosed in the proxy statement.[1] This is a very useful prescription. Board members attending such meetings are likely to talk with one another more frankly than they would if the CEOs and/or other managers were present. If the name of the presiding director is made public, readers of the proxy statement are more likely to feel reassured that "all's well" on the governance front. The independent directors are meeting alone and are *"on top of things,"* is the expected reaction.

But it could be false comfort. In reality, no one—except the directors in attendance—will ever find out whether or not the meetings are actually serving their intended purpose. The behavior of the board members cannot be controlled from outside the boardroom. The directors might meet for a few minutes or many hours. They may or may not deal with significant matters. Their leader may or may not have a deep grasp of the issues or the skill to help them reach a consensus. As important as such a new requirement is, all that it can do is give boards the opportunity to do the right thing. What actually happens behind the closed doors depends upon the directors in the room.

Directors who truly want to build an effective board need to look far beyond any externally imposed rules and procedures. The starting point is taking an honest look at how—and how well—they work with one another. An effective board is both supportive and challenging of management, and reaches consensus while encouraging dissent—balances that are hard to achieve. In this chapter, we look at what often goes wrong among board members behind closed doors, and what patterns of behavior are most desirable. And as we focus on board behavior, we must remind ourselves that how board members act together is not random. As we have argued throughout, the behavior of board members is determined by the design of each board: its membership, its structure and process, and its culture.

Boardroom Misbehavior

THERE ARE a number of things that can go wrong behind the closed doors of a boardroom, and through our work with boards and in discussions with hundreds of directors and senior executives, we can say with some confidence that we really have seen them all. Some common examples:

- *The CEO is defensive and not open with the board.* As a result, discussions often become tense and questioning difficult. The directors feel inhibited and withhold their opinions.

- *Management presents poorly organized material to the board, or simply reports each decision as a fait accompli.* As a result, the board is left without the opportunity to explore alternative courses of action.

- *The directors feel their contributions aren't sought or valued.* This can lead to a passive board, where directors "turn off" and don't even try to make a contribution.

- *Directors use the meeting to score points with each other, perhaps to prove that they are very wise or have read their board reports. Or, they take up time describing how wonderfully things are done in other companies where they have experience.* As a result, board discussions become "performances" that fail to tackle the issues critical to the company.

- *When management reports bad news (and all companies have some of that) board members "shoot the messenger."* As a result, such news comes more slowly in the future, and often too late for corrective action.

- *Directors talk a lot, but listen much less. They expect to be treated with deference, and their "conversations" with executives are mostly one-way.* As a result, directors don't have their own views tested adequately, and don't learn what managers know and think.

- *The CEO consistently monopolizes the meeting time telling directors what has been happening in the company and the industry.* As a result, too little time is left for other agenda items and for discussion among board members.

- *The independent directors' "executive sessions" are disorganized and lengthy.* As a result, board members are frustrated at the wasted time, and the CEO is left in a state of rising anxiety and, at least figuratively, is pacing the floor. "What are they doing in there?"

- *The chairman is overly concerned about finishing meetings on time.* As a result, important discussions are truncated; the last items on the agenda are discussed in haste as directors close their briefcases and head for the door. Often, as we have said, this problem is exacerbated by an overly full agenda.

- *The CEO and chairman (or CEO and lead director, when the former chairs the board) have no agreement on the activities each should undertake.* Consequently, the content of the agenda may not be well planned, and the independent directors are confused about who is playing what part in leading the board deliberations.

- *Directors deal with the CEO's subordinates by contacting them directly and without alerting the CEO. Alternatively, directors believe they should have no interactions with the CEO's direct reports because they know she disapproves of such contact.* In the first case, directors might undermine the CEO's relationship with his subordinates. In the second, directors remain ignorant about what the executive team is thinking.

This lengthy list reflects the difficulty of the board's task. It also reflects a root cause of ineffective (or detrimental) board behavior: To be effective, a board *must constructively manage two sets of relationships: one among the board members themselves and one between the directors and senior managers, particularly the CEO.* Every board must deal with this web of relationships in which problems can become self-reinforcing and hard to fix.

Without a pattern of behavior that avoids the kinds of problems we have just listed and that nurtures productive working relationships, directors find it difficult, if not impossible, to accomplish anything meaningful in their limited time together. In the balance of this chapter, we explore ways in which the right behavior is most likely to be encouraged.

The "Right" Boardroom Behavior

A S WE'VE NOTED, most directors are successful and high-status women and men, responsible for very important institutions. They oversee thousands of employees and billions of dollars in assets, and their responsibilities are defined both by law and by stakeholders' expectations. And although they meet in private, their decisions are often scrutinized and criticized in the public arena; as a result, they risk damage to their reputations—and even legal repercussions—when things go wrong. Reduced to their essentials, though, boards are simply small groups of people who accomplish most of their work when they meet, periodically, face-to-face. That fact makes relevant a rich array of research and thinking about any high-level decision-making group.

While the design factors we have been discussing will determine how such groups function, we want to focus on two important influences on the behavior of board members in their meetings. *First,* and most obvious, is the behavior of the group's leader, the chairman. He has the greatest control over the scarcest resource—time. He determines whose views are given most emphasis, what issues will be discussed, how much time will be devoted to each, and in what order. He determines the allocation of time between presentations and discussions, as well as how disagreements are resolved.

The norms that evolve in any group are the second important factor that we want to consider here. They define the behaviors that members see as appropriate or otherwise. These norms are affected by the board's design: the characteristics of its members, the leadership structure, the number of meetings and their length, etc. They develop throughout the history of the group as its members interact and work together. New directors learn about them as they attend their first meetings, simply by observing more experienced board members' behavior. In this way they gain an understanding of which behaviors are seen as okay and which are implicitly frowned upon. One example of what a new board member will learn is how much she should speak up and express a counterpoint view at meetings. All the boards we know have unwritten rules about this. If a novice director begins to take up too much of the board's "air time," the more experienced directors will signal their displeasure in subtle ways. The experienced directors implicitly understand their board's norms and find ways to reinforce them, subtly at first, and more overtly if that does not work. Even successful and powerful people are sensitive to this kind of group pressure.

A board's set of norms—some would call this the board's culture—is a powerful driver of directors' behavior. It tends to determine who sits where, how to behave if meetings fall behind schedule, and which directors' opinions deserve respect. If, as is often the case, the person seated at the head of the board table has no conscious awareness of these norms, he will find it difficult to change them, if change is needed, to channel the group's interactions in more productive directions.

Boards clearly need leaders who are sensitive to the existing group norms and who are also able, over time, to help the group develop norms that encourage productive behaviors. What's more, boards need leaders who will not hesitate to "name" those preferred behaviors; to do otherwise is to leave too much to chance. Further, effective leaders must be able to comprehend how the board's design is getting in the way of the desired behaviors or encouraging them. Here are the minimum requisite behaviors:

- Directors can ask tough questions without management becoming defensive.

- Dissent among directors is encouraged, and pressures for conformity to the majority opinion are acknowledged and guarded against.

- Directors aren't intent on scoring points by putting managers or other directors down. Instead, they engage in discussions of relevant issues, with respect for each other's opinions and expertise, and with the goal of reaching understanding and consensus.

- Directors understand when to listen and learn from management and each other, and when to stimulate discussions.

- Any discussion between executives and directors is two-way. Executives can disagree with directors if they believe the latter are misinformed or wrong, and directors really listen to management's ideas.

- Directors respect the agenda. They are mindful of the schedule and understand the importance of staying focused on the important issues. Discussion is encouraged, but everyone recognizes the limits imposed by time.

If norms like these develop in a boardroom, not only will directors feel more comfortable contributing, but the chairman's job will also become easier. Her goal of encouraging productive and open discussion, and resolving conflicting opinions, will be supported by her fellow directors' behavior. Even with this advantage, the chairman will still have a significant task. She must encourage participation while keeping an eye on the clock, and in a way that ensures that real issues get onto the table. Importantly, she must press for clarity on the decisions that have been reached, and test for real consensus. This requires more than a count of hands or a formal vote. It involves understanding what directors truly think.

Encouraging the Preferred Behaviors

O F C O U R S E , agreeing to a list of desired behaviors is just the starting point. Once the board has explicitly made clear what are—and are not—desirable director norms, then the chairman must follow through by managing board meetings and other interactions so those norms will be supported, and undesirable behavior discouraged. As well, each director must take the next step to help the board move from agreeing, intellectually, that certain behaviors are desirable, and actually practicing those behaviors. The board must build the new norms into the way in which it works, and be sure the board's design is supportive of these behaviors.

As we have said, a good board is supportive and challenging of management, and the behaviors that support this cannot be left to chance. Here are a few good ways to encourage this behavior:

- *Clarify the relationship directors seek—and need—with the CEO and the senior executive team:* Boards must decide whether the relationship they want is like that of a boss and subordinate, or more akin to a partnership.

- *Build "constructive dissent" into the board process itself:* Boards must take steps to make sure that ideas are thoroughly challenged, because there are many pressures that work to stop this from happening. Important here is ensuring that the board has adequate time and information for such conversations.

- *Acknowledge the tensions implicit in the director's relationship with management, a relationship that has to permit "due diligence" while preserving "trust":* Both are important, but they will often work against each other in counterproductive ways.

- *"Use the thermometer":* That is, periodically measure the board's behavior through the evaluation techniques discussed in chapter 6. It's an effective way to keep nudging practice in the desired direction.

Working with the CEO

We've highlighted a few ways in which independent directors can work more effectively with their colleagues from management. But the relationship between the directors and the CEO is worth exploring in more detail. As we have said, directors must be clear about the type of relationship they seek with the senior executive team. What is it currently? Is it a boss and subordinate-type relationship or is it more of a partnership? Should it be one or the other? (Is it, in fact, currently what the board members perceive it to be?)

Directors have traditionally liked to think of themselves in the "boss" role. Indeed, in the worst-case examples, directors have expected to be treated as if they were royalty, and never openly challenged. Even in well-functioning boards, executives' readiness to disagree with directors has often been circumscribed. As well, the architecture and furnishing of many boardrooms is intended to convey a sense of awe and prestige—to intimidate rather than foster open, productive working relationships. And post-Enron, boards are again being urged to "take control," to assert their authority.

But although it's true that the board has the ultimate legal authority, the reality is much more complex. In many respects, the power relationship is actually the reverse, with the CEO in the driver's seat, despite appearances. After all, a board can only be effective if the CEO wants it to be so. It is only when boards grasp this fact that they can truly function effectively and have the power to govern.

We're not suggesting that directors simply bow to the wishes of management, go home, and call it a day. Rather, we'd like them to answer the following question: "To what extent can we do our job without the active assistance and support of the CEO and her team?" It's a simple question, but many boards will find the answer disturbing, because it will expose their dependence on their CEO and confront them with the true complexity of their relationship with her.

Yes, the board will ultimately prevail over the CEO if there is a battle. But equally, while the CEO is in place, the directors are overwhelmingly dependent on him for planning their meetings and providing the information and knowledge they need. Our point? The board and CEO must work together as partners. There really is no other way!

The notion that the directors and management must relate to each other as partners in the leadership of the company will not sit easily with many governance activists who see the board's role in more black and white terms, as keeping management under control. But directors who understand that management has many levers of power will approach their task in a very different way from those who believe that they hold most of the power in the relationship. A board that understands this will encourage executives to express their sometimes contrary views rather than expect them to stay silent until they are spoken to. It will reward rather than punish early disclosure of bad news. The board will listen and observe very carefully rather than be content to heed only its own opinions.

In this sense boards embody an interesting paradox. *They are simultaneously among the most and the least hierarchal institutions in the business world.*

Consider that the board itself is supposed to be, and in reality often is, a collegial body in which each director is individually and jointly accountable for the board's work. At least in theory, there is an almost complete absence of formal hierarchy within the board. No director's opinion is supposed to be more important than another's. Even the chairman is supposed to deal with other directors as peers. In fact, the directors formally elect their chairman. They operate very much as would a genuine partnership.

At the same time, the board sits at the pinnacle of its company's organization structure, right at the top of the company hierarchy. At least in theory, it is the body from which all power flows. In every country of which we are aware, the law makes it clear that the board is the boss and the CEO works for it.

However, as we have seen, the power relationship between the CEO and the board is not a straightforward one. In the ordinary course of affairs, a CEO has quite a few ways to influence the effectiveness of his company's board. The CEOs we surveyed understand this very well (see appendix, Proposition E-6). Most of them believe the board's success depends on them—that a board can only be as effective as the CEO wants it to be.

The survey results match what we know from our own experience. In the United States and other countries where the chairman and CEO are the same person, the CEO almost always has considerable influence over the board. The CEO plans the board agenda, provides the board with information about the company (through his management team), and sits at the head of the board table to moderate board meetings. The board may legally be in charge, but the CEO can do a great deal to hinder or facilitate the board's work.

Even when the chairman and CEO are different people, the latter has a very significant role in the board's work, because she knows the issues that require discussion. She works with the chairman to plan the agenda and is also the source of virtually all of the information provided to the board. She may appear to have less influence on the board than her peers in the United States, but she still has a considerable impact on the board's effectiveness. Without her active assistance, the board will struggle to know what is going on and which issues need to be addressed.

We encourage directors to name the relationship they seek with management. Is it to be a boss and subordinate relationship with the CEO and her senior team? Or, legal issues aside, is the desired relationship more like one of peers working together? We understand that there are some circumstances in which the boss/subordinate relationship might seem to be desirable, particularly if the board feels it cannot trust the CEO to live up to the level of transparency required for a partner relationship. But if that is the case, we would recommend that the board move quickly to replace the CEO with someone who can work—and thrive—in a relationship that plays out on a level field. A hierarchical relationship, over the long term, is simply not in the best interests of the company. Indeed, it is symptomatic of a board—and an executive team—that is not performing to its potential.

Legitimized Dissent

One of the most challenging issues boards face is how to ensure that dissenting views are heard and assessed. Group norms can discourage such dissent, and the chairman may be tempted to go along with this, given the pressures to reach consensus quickly.

Even when the climate around the board table is amenable to dissent, it is worth exploring whether a process is in place to ensure that all angles are canvassed. Many directors quickly reach a point where they feel they should not continue questioning a proposal. There can be pressure from a defensive management team to curb the probing. The other directors might have lost interest. Even when she has lingering doubts, a director in this position might simply shut up because she doesn't want to violate the board's norms and offend her peers. This can be a particular danger for a board whose company has been successful for many years. We have all seen instances where very successful companies have suddenly hit difficulties and failed. Some directors of some of those companies may well have decided not to rock the boat, even though they saw problems on the horizon.

The pressure on directors to acquiesce to the majority opinion increases as a meeting progresses. Most want to be supportive of management and to avoid wasting time. Individual directors often feel they have used up their allocation of this scarce commodity after asking two or three hard questions. Think back to the first of the two directors quoted at the opening of this chapter; he felt that after a few questions, he was becoming a nuisance. Many of his peers share that view. The problem, of course, is that if they stop asking questions or expressing doubts when they are still unconvinced, the board could make a poor decision that further discussion would have exposed.

To avoid outcomes like these, boards need to put in place mechanisms that enable directors to challenge management without creating resentment and conflict. We call the process of doing so "legitimizing dissent." One way of doing it is to establish a temporary board committee (like the special committees described in chapter 5) to deal with "bet the business" decisions. Another option is to appoint what one board called a "designated critic" role for each particularly large and important decision, asking one or two directors to critically examine a major proposal. While all the directors are expected to pursue the issues as they see fit, the designated critics are expected to go the extra mile in learning about and questioning the deal.

The designated critic (or special committee) can ask any number of questions and pick away at the weak points of an argument without being seen as a troublemaker or a pedant. This is because the role has been defined—it is what the rest of the directors and management expect. We believe the logic is unarguable. Directors who want to be supportive of management and are generally satisfied with management's performance can easily become soft in their questioning. By legitimizing dissent, boards will ensure that important decisions attract robust debate without creating the ill feeling that too many difficult questions can engender.

A similar approach was used in at least one publicized case at GE when Jack Welch was at the helm. Managers were instructed to prepare the case for how Internet businesses might destroy their own businesses. In other words, they were instructed to develop the "no" case in an environment where organization pressures could well have blocked serious consideration of the idea. Dispassionate development and examination of both the pro and con cases will always lead to better decision making, no matter what the endeavor. If this is not done at the board level, the risk is that arguments solidify around the pro case that management advocates, and the social pressures against criticism become immense.

We have had some success in persuading directors that legitimized dissent is a sensible idea when bet the business decisions are on the table, although many directors are reluctant to embrace the idea. Perhaps they find it hard to admit that their normal probing sometimes falls short of what is needed. Certainly, we find that boards are more prepared to experiment in this area when they carry the scars from previous, well-remembered failures. Just ask any director whose board approved an acquisition that subsequently failed.

Due Diligence and Trust

Access to information is critical to the board's effectiveness, but we sometimes see management and directors working at cross-purposes. Management believes it is entitled to be trusted and has clear views on what the board needs to know. On the other hand, the board believes that its due diligence role means that directors must question management beyond the information it provides.

The real power dynamics between the board and management means that a productive working relationship between the directors and the top management team is both critically important and complicated to achieve. Our surveyed CEOs overwhelmingly believe their boards deal with them constructively, but this is only half the equation (see appendix, Proposition B-8). A good board must not only support management, it must also challenge it. To do both, a board must have an open and trusting relationship with its CEO and his senior colleagues. The responsibilities of both parties must be crystal clear. Neither should sidestep difficult issues, but must instead confront and resolve them, though it is anything but easy. Considerable skill and wisdom are required. Powerful egos are involved and significant careers are at stake.

There is, of course, much that can go wrong. In one company we know, the CEO believed that, having agreed to the plans and budgets, the board should be satisfied with regular management reports and only receive supplementary information if a significant variation occurred. No additional news was to be seen as good news. The CEO's position was very clear. Beyond the usual board information, there was no need for the board to engage in further digging. His attitude could be defined as, "I will tell you immediately if there is anything you need to know."

Some of this company's directors had a different view. They believed they had a clear responsibility to constantly make sure that management was doing its job. One director, whose vigorous questioning of the management might have reflected his legal training, described his role as, "I ask questions and demand information to satisfy my due diligence obligations. It has nothing to do with trust." But the senior executives didn't share this view. This director's questioning had become a serious irritant, and they believed he had no trust in their abilities.

The tensions in this board festered for a long time. The problem was seen as a clash of styles and personalities. What was actually happening was a conflict between two legitimate approaches to disclosing information that had become confused with questions of trust. Because the different views of what information should be provided to directors had not surfaced, the board and management were often at odds. Different assumptions about information sharing lie at the heart of many misunderstandings in board and management relationships, but they are rarely identified and even less frequently dealt with.

Boards and management sometimes forget that, ultimately, they are on the same team. In the throes of conflicting styles and pressures to perform, that's easy to do. But it is critically important to continually try to recognize that each party has a valid position—they each have a job to do. Management must understand that directors are obligated to dig deep into important issues. On the other hand, directors must concede that they can at best scratch the surface of complicated issues in their due diligence efforts (even the top management cannot have a totally informed understanding of what lies deep inside the company). Ultimately, the security of the business depends on candor and openness at all levels of the company. If this isn't demonstrated at the top between the board and the senior executive team, it will not be replicated below. The board has to trust management because it has no alternative. Management has to accept that directors must dig into the matters before it. Directors must encourage and reward early disclosure of problems. They have a serious obligation to cultivate an atmosphere of trust in which full and early disclosure is encouraged, from the shop floor right up to the boardroom.

Use the Thermometer

Certainly, a board that has been well designed is highly likely to have members who are themselves trustworthy, straightforward, and more than willing to contribute whatever it takes to add value to the company.

But as we've said, the strengths of the individual directors aren't the issue about which we are concerned here; rather, it is how they function as a group. Understanding this can't be left to chance. We need a way to stimulate boards to assess and possibly alter their behavior, as well as their relationship with their CEO and his team. To that end, as suggested in chapter 6, we believe that every board should, at least every two years, undertake a review of how well it is functioning. As part of this, there should be an explicit review of the board's behavior. In figure 8-1, we suggest ten questions that might provide the basis for such an appraisal. These questions go to the heart of board behavior. They provide a checklist (perhaps scored on a one to five scale) for a health audit of a board's behavior, and therefore of its leadership and norms. Not only directors but also the most senior executives should be involved in this review, because they, too, see the board in action.

These questions are useful in highlighting subtle but important behavior issues. For example, question four about whether the CEO

FIGURE 8 - 1

Ten Questions for Assessing Board Behavior

1. Is the chairman's leadership style effective?

2. Do the chairman (or lead director) and CEO have a good working relationship?

3. Do the chairman (or lead director) and CEO understand their respective roles?

4. Does the CEO encourage contributions from the board?

5. Is the relationship between directors and management a constructive one?

6. Are there agreed procedures for contact between management and directors outside board meetings?

7. Can individual directors raise issues for discussion without difficulty—in other words, is dissent OK?

8. Do directors express their views to each other and to management in ways that are constructive?

9. Having reached decisions, are directors cohesive in supporting the board's decision?

10. Is bad news communicated quickly and openly by management to the board?

---

seeks contributions from the board always draws out any concerns directors have about their roles. And answers to question ten about bad news reveal whether lack of trust or executive spin is perceived to be a problem. If such problems are brought to light, they can be nipped in the bud before they become destructive. In addition, answers to these questions signal the types of behaviors and relationships that directors value and see as productive. The desired standard is clearly articulated and always on display.

Altering Behavior

WHAT HAPPENS behind the closed doors of a boardroom is the key determinant of how effective boards can be. The behaviors we have described—candor, trust, robust discussion and debate, and legitimate dissent—should be the norm in every boardroom and in every interaction among directors and between directors and managers.

So if board members find they do not have this pattern of behavior, what can be done? We believe that is the critical moment to go back to the drawing board and revamp the board's design. The first step is to try to identify the causes of the errant behavior. Ask:

- Does it occur because of the persistent actions of one or a few directors?

- Do we need to provide personal feedback or perhaps replace one or two of the members?

- Does the problem lie in the board's structure? Does the board need different behavior from its chairman? If the chairman and CEO are the same person, would a lead director help to resolve the problem?

- Do the causes of the difficulty stem from the board's use of time? Are we trying to cram too much onto each agenda, so that discussions are truncated and inconclusive? Do we need more meeting time? Should we consider doing more work in committees, or even to create additional committees?

- Do the causes lie in the amount or quality of knowledge and information that the board has about its company? Do we need to improve the flow of information to directors? Would it help to add a director or two who is familiar with our industry?

These are examples of the kinds of questions boards need to explore when behavior goes awry. In our experience, the problems are likely to have multiple causes. Going back to the drawing board requires an examination of all the design elements we have discussed. Remember, behavior in the boardroom, or for any decision-making group, is determined by the interaction of the system of design variables we have discussed throughout the book. Improving behavior requires examining all aspects of the board's design and then adjusting those components that are causing the difficulties.

nine

Getting Down to Work

B OARDS ARE A CONUNDRUM. TAKE A GROUP OF PART-
time directors and present them with an extremely difficult job, but give them very limited time together. And then charge this
institution with ultimate responsibility for ensuring that the nation's
most important economic assets are well managed. How can such an
unlikely arrangement work?

It works *only because of the commitment of the women and men who
serve as directors*. That's why, in this concluding chapter, we're going to
get personal. The challenge going forward is to drive the changes necessary to make tomorrow's boards more effective than today's. We want
to talk about what you, as individual board members, need to do to implement the changes we've been proposing.

We shall examine the key challenges facing boards from the perspectives of the various board members themselves: the independent
directors, the inside or management directors, and the leaders in the
boardroom—the CEO and/or board chairman, the "lead director" in
those boards where the same person serves as CEO *and* chairman of

the board, and those who lead the board committees. Whatever your role, you should read them all. If boards are truly going to improve, all of the directors must work together to make the needed changes.

Independent Directors

W E'LL START with independent directors, because you are going to be the majority occupants of boardrooms in the future.

The key to maintaining your independence rests in the idea of the entire board being independent. You must deliberately set out to develop practices and a culture that emphasize and value independence. You and your independent peers, in other words, must achieve a strong sense of identity as a group. Among the prerequisites for making this happen are having an independent leader, and making sure the independent directors meet alone from time to time. The message you'll send is: "We are an independent body. We can respect and even be fond of management and the company, but we must maintain our independent perspective." Independence must become a state of mind that permeates the boardroom.

From time to time, you may find that another obligation, whether it is your previous or primary employment or another board seat, creates a conflict of interest. The solution is to recognize the conflict, acknowledge it outright, and excuse yourself from discussions and decisions where the conflict could be an issue.

If you represent a significant shareholder, you face a particular problem. You have a natural concern for your own investment, but you also have a duty to the other shareholders as well. If there is a conflict between the interests of the shareholder you represent and the broader shareholders, again recognize and explain the potential conflict to your fellow board members and then, if you or they feel there is a conflict, excuse yourself from relevant discussions and decisions. This does not, of course, preclude your articulating to the full board the actions that you believe to be in the interest of the owners you represent. This is a right all shareholders should have.

What about the issues of knowledge and time? By joining the board as an independent director, you have agreed that you will make the commitment to do the job right. You will have a long list of board responsibilities and, as a part-timer with a demanding life outside the board, you will find it difficult to manage the trade-off between the time you have available to spend on board duties and the knowledge you need to perform your role effectively. This means thinking carefully before you join a board about the time that is going to be required. Board membership means attending regularly scheduled meetings; it also means having separate conversations with the CEO and other directors between meetings. What's more, we know of no board where unanticipated problems and crises do not occur. Do you have the time and flexibility to drop your normal responsibilities to address such issues in specially called meetings or as a member of an ad hoc committee?

Consider what one director told us about being involved in an ad hoc search committee for a new CEO with two other directors. Over a six-month period he had to cancel many other obligations to attend meetings of the committee to meet possible candidates. This was in addition to the evenings and weekends spent on conference calls with the other two committee members. Ultimately, he estimated he spent the equivalent of twelve days of his time on this work. This is as much time as the typical U.S. director spends annually on all his work for *one* board.

Remember, too, that your job as a director is only going to become more complex and demanding. If today you are spending between ten and fifteen days a year on board business, tomorrow you are likely to have to increase that number significantly. When the business is in trouble or undergoing substantial change, you will need to spend even more time.

A related challenge is to make the best use of your time, in particular how you build and maintain knowledge about the company you are serving. It is your responsibility to keep learning about the company and its important issues. The deeper your knowledge, the more effective you'll be. Talk to the chairman and your director colleagues about "learning" experiences—presentations from executives or outside experts. If the orientation sessions you participated in when you joined the board were helpful, ask for some refresher sessions each year. Beyond the information you routinely receive, be proactive and try to spend more time between board meetings engaged with company executives and other participants in the industry (being careful not to undermine your CEO as you do so). If your management has retained outside experts in areas of interest to the board, make an effort to hear what they have to say. Familiarize yourself with some of the company's operations. Get to know up-and-coming executives. Learn about competitors and how customers see the company through conversations with managers, industry publications, trade shows, and analyst reports. Understand what the investment community is saying about your company.

Don't assume you must only be a generalist. Your time is heavily constrained, and unless you and your colleagues share the burden, your collective understanding of the company will be superficial at best. Agree to a special area of interest with the chairman and your fellow directors, and become especially knowledgeable about it. You will be surprised how much you learn about the company as a whole while exploring a narrow slice of it.

You probably receive a mountain of material in your board "books," but how much of it sticks? Determine what you really need to know and check your list against the one we included in chapter 7. Encourage management to redesign the board information if you find important gaps in what is provided, but don't waste valuable management time on "fishing expeditions" to find information that is of personal interest to you but not central to the board's work. Ascertain whether computer technology can give you immediate and continual access to better information, including some stored on selected company databases that you can tap into.

It goes without saying that you should accept the need for board evaluations and that your board has a right—and a duty—to rid itself of directors who are not doing the job and to critically assess how the board as a whole is working. You can't sit at the top of a well-performing company and exempt yourself from performance review. Your renomination to the board should also be subject to review and the endorsement of your fellow independent directors.

As far as navigating the waters of group dynamics goes, give careful thought to how you should be involved in board discussions. Ask as many questions as you feel you must, but remember that you are part of a team. Have a quiet discussion with the chairman after the meeting if you think you are being ignored or not getting the answers you're looking for. Always treat the executives with respect. Encourage early disclosure of problems, and never shoot the messenger.

If you don't press for answers when you have an uneasy feeling in the pit of your stomach that something isn't right, you'll end up like a number of directors we know saying, "All my instincts said there were unresolved problems in that business, but I was anxious to get on to the other matters on the agenda so we'd finish the meeting on time."

Most important and more broadly, think through the relationship that you want with management and with your board colleagues. Finding the sweet spot isn't all that easy. Obviously you can't be a rubber stamp and meet the considerable expectations that directors now face. On the other hand, if you throw your weight around in an aggressive way, you're unlikely to have a productive working relationship with management or your fellow directors. You need to be a positive contributor to board discussions—putting forth your ideas, but also listening to the views of your colleagues. There is nothing wrong, and a lot right, about stating your views strongly and clearly. But also try hard to listen carefully to your colleagues; when others have the more convincing arguments, it will not reflect badly on you if you back off gracefully.

Remember, too, that your board can only be effective if the CEO wants it to be, whether you like it or not. Ask yourself periodically whether you believe that the CEO is open with the board. If the answer is "no," insist that the issue be addressed in discussions among the independent directors. The problem might be the CEO's, but it could also be the board's. If it lies with the CEO, the board needs to press for candor. If he won't change, move to replace him. If you can't achieve that, resign from the board; in such a scenario, the board is too dangerous a place to be.

Finally, be warned! When companies fail, the view in hindsight is almost always that the directors failed to see the "obvious" signs of impending disaster. How can you guarantee that you smell the smoke under the door before the business burns down? Or at least improve your chances of spotting a potential crisis? Ask yourself: Do you and other directors challenge your company's strategic direction in board meetings before small problems become big ones? Are you alert to signals like missed plans and budgets, acquisitions that never work out, risk management failures, loss of market share to competitors, and inadequate staff development? Do you recognize when these add up to a pattern requiring board action? If not, your chances of averting disaster before it strikes are low.

The truth is that in most instances, it's very difficult for individual directors to "smell the smoke," much less put out the fire before it spreads. Nonetheless, that task is central to the board's work, and you need to have a frank discussion among the independent directors and with the CEO about what you must understand to be able to recognize problems before they're out of control. As independent directors, you are in the best position to take a dispassionate view of your company, but you need to work hard to gain the information to do so.

In our experience, many company failures could have been averted if worried directors had spoken frankly to each other about their concerns. Many people sitting around the board table sensed that many little problems were leading to big ones. But there were never discussions among the independent directors to allow them to share their concerns and learn if there really was a fire that needed to be extinguished.

Inside (Executive) Directors

A S AN INSIDE DIRECTOR, you're in the minority on most boards, but we see no reason to believe you're going to go the way of the dinosaur. Instead, we believe many boards (and shareholders) will continue to choose to elect one or a few members of management (in addition to the CEO) to their board.

If you are a company executive and you get a seat at the board table, it is essential to remember that you are equal to everyone else on the board. You should not have been asked to occupy this board seat as a reward for past performance. If you believe you've been selected for any other reason than your potential to contribute to the board like all the other directors, then our advice is to resign quickly, because it won't work, and you will find yourself in an untenable position.

Let's assume that you were selected because you have something important to contribute. You still have a unique problem among board members. Your boss, the CEO, is also in the room and possibly sitting at the head of the table. It's going to be hard to express your own opinions and to take a position that's different from his. This problem is your own test of independence, and the solution is quite straightforward. Before agreeing to join the board, you must sit down with the CEO and reach an understanding that, when wearing your board-member hat, you must be free to express your own ideas even when they differ from his. You must both agree that you have the same responsibility and rights as your peers; in the boardroom you cannot act as a subordinate. But you also should recognize your responsibility to maintain a dialogue with the CEO between board meetings about any disagreements, and how to use those disagreements to promote constructive discussion among the board as a whole.

Having reached this agreement, you should feel less inhibited about joining in board discussions—and you will have much to contribute. You are more knowledgeable than your independent peers and you can use that knowledge to enhance their understanding.

Remember that as a full-fledged director, you have a duty to protect your fellow board members against a situation where the CEO misleads or puts too much "spin" on his description of what is happening in the company. Be clear that your ultimate duty is to the board and the company. If you feel that the board is being consistently and deliberately misled, you are obviously in a difficult situation. Ultimately, however, having accepted your board seat, you must inform the chairman (if not the CEO) or the lead director of your concerns.

One group of independent directors we know debated about whether or not to fire the company's CEO in one-on-one conversations and in "executive sessions." After six months, they did, in fact, fire him. Subsequently, the company's remaining inside director admitted that he had known about the problems that led to his boss's downfall for over a year, but felt he shouldn't say anything out of loyalty. All he could do at that late date was apologize to his fellow directors.

Of course you should excuse yourself from meetings when you have a conflict of interest, the most obvious of which will be the evaluation of the CEO and issues of management compensation and management succession. Again, it is best to be clear in advance about what these issues are, not only with the CEO/chairman but also with the other board members. In short, be explicit with all the directors about the role you can and will play.

Board Leaders: The Chairman and the CEO

As CHAIRMAN and/or CEO, you have the most important roles on the board. Any failures in governance will invariably be attributed to you. You set the tone in the boardroom as well as control the agenda, and you determine what information the board will review. As we have said, the board cannot succeed if you do not want it to.

Whether you are the chairman or CEO or both, your responsibility to the board is to ensure its effectiveness. This includes leading the board in thinking through its role and design. Decisions about these two critical issues will ultimately be driven by how much the board needs to understand about the business, how the company is performing, and how much time board members can devote to their duties. Most boards don't talk about these things or make conscious decisions about them. It's up to you to make sure that your company's board does.

Aside from this all-important leadership task, how you should behave will depend on whether or not you are both the chairman *and* the

CEO. Let's start with the situation in which the jobs are split between two people.

Both of you need to be clear about your individual duties and responsibilities. In theory, the CEO is the leader of the company and its management, and the chairman is the leader of the board. It sounds simple, but we have seen too many instances where there is confused overlap or even conflict. It is essential that the two of you have a clear understanding about who is going to do what. This might get tricky, because the dividing line between the board and management roles is vague.

If, for example, you are chairman, how active do you want to be in offering advice to your CEO, or in approving his decisions? If you are CEO, how involved do you want the chairman to be? Do you report to the chairman individually or to the board as a whole? What is the role of each party in setting board agendas? Clearly it is the chairman's job to finalize the agenda, but the CEO must have significant involvement, since he is most knowledgeable about the issues that need board input and/or decisions. It's up to you both to reach agreement on matters like these, to clearly articulate your preferred working relationship to each other and to the board, and to see that it works year in and year out. If you don't have a clear understanding and agreement all around about your respective responsibilities, you are headed for trouble, and so is the board.

If you are in the other situation—both board chairman and CEO—let's be honest, you face an inherent conflict. You are like the fox in the chicken coop, and there is no point in denying it. In essence, you are trying to lead the board, which is there to oversee your performance as CEO, determine your compensation, and in the end, decide your tenure.

If you took these two leadership positions because you like complex challenges, you made the right choice! Now you have to figure out how to do both simultaneously. Our advice? First, be clear with yourself about how complicated your situation really is. Having the two titles, chairman and CEO, may feel great and keep you in the same league as your peers in comparable companies, especially in the United States, but if you don't recognize the need to work through the complex web of relationships in which you find yourself, you, your board, or both could fail.

You need to accept that the independent directors must have a leader drawn from their number. The days of resisting this are pretty much over. Understand that this is correct in principle, and put your effort into making it work in practice. The title doesn't matter—lead director, presiding director, even a committee chairman. What does matter is that such a designated leader exists, selected by the independent directors, and accepted as legitimate by all the directors, including you. And the outside world is entitled to know who this person is.

So don't be like one CEO/chairman we encountered who reluctantly agreed to accept the idea of having a lead director as long as he could select him, and as long as there was no public disclosure. Needless to say, the tension between the CEO and the lead director was palpable, and the latter carried out his job on tiptoe.

Obviously you need to work with the lead director to define his duties and their relation to your job as chairman, and you will have to do this at a time when defining the demarcation between your respective roles, even in best practice boards, is still in a state of flux. From our perspective, this leader is not there to supplant you as chairman but rather to lead the board when you cannot or should not. We will talk more about the lead director's job shortly. At this point, we just want to emphasize our belief that it is a relatively specific, narrow job, so it's important that all board members reach a consensus on this, including you and the lead director. You'll need to revisit your understanding with the lead director regularly and make sure you understand how your board colleagues judge the arrangements.

Since the chairman (whether it's the CEO or not) is responsible for the board's effectiveness, you periodically should lead the board in a review of its design and performance. In this review, here are some issues to keep in mind. Keep the board small, but ensure that it represents an appropriate mix of skills and experience. Think about the portfolio of skills your company needs; the corporate governance committee should have input from all the directors on the skill gaps that should be filled when it's time to make a new nomination. Explore whether the board should consider having some directors who are not independent but who bring valuable knowledge to the board. Encourage the independent directors to own this issue, because they must feel comfortable about the appointment of any outside directors who don't satisfy current definitions of "independence."

Be certain you understand how the board members feel about the information they are getting. Is it adequate for them to do their job? If not, what changes should be made? You also need to ensure that the board members have assessed the way the board is carrying out its most significant duties of oversight, decision making, and giving advice. Is the board playing its intended role? Are the practices used for deciding about and reviewing strategy and for evaluating the CEO and overseeing management succession working well? If not, what changes are needed? Are the board's committees working well? Remember, you're not responsible for answering all these questions by yourself. Your job is to get the other directors to reach a consensus about them. Then you can encourage any needed change.

The review of board performance must include some feedback to you on how you are carrying out your job as chairman. One of the other directors—the lead director or the chairman of the corporate governance committee—should be given the task of collecting feedback from the other directors and the senior executive group. This is an opportunity for you to set an example to the organization; if you aren't interested in doing your job better, why should anyone else in the company care about being evaluated?

Don't put up with directors who perform modestly at best. Be prepared to tackle the issue of moving them out. Such directors don't just drag down the board's performance; the company's executive team knows who the poor performers are, and it reflects poorly on you and the board if they continue to occupy a board seat. Executives are expected to deal with poor performers, and boards should be, too, despite the difficulties this sometimes poses.

Let's be candid. Removing a director is never a pleasant task. Yet in our experience, when the director in question is confronted honestly and told that his colleagues are concerned about his contribution, there is often a sense of relief—a feeling of, "I know you guys aren't happy with me, so maybe it's best if we part company." In such instances, honesty is the best policy.

While we are on the subject of performance, take some time to think about how to motivate the other directors. Many chairmen seem to assume that all directors will be self-motivated to perform at their best. Not so. As we have said, most directors serve because they feel they will learn from doing so. But serving and being motivated to do your best are two different things. Learning, prestige, and money might be enough to motivate some directors, but most of us need something more. Directors truly want to feel that they are making a contribution. They want to feel useful. As the board's leader, you must keep the board engaged in its task. Draw them all into board discussions and make sure they feel free to ask questions, probe issues, and contribute ideas. Your directors are much more likely to go the extra mile if they feel engaged. Your job, like that of any leader, is to create an environment that brings out the best in your people. If too many directors are sitting passively on the sidelines, you need to examine your own leadership approach.

The way you act in the chair can promote frank and honest discussion, or the opposite. Encourage constructive dissent so that important ("bet the business") decisions can be fully tested without rancor. You may even want to design such dissent into the board's process. Keep in mind the special committees we discussed in chapter 5.

Bill George, who was chairman and CEO of Medtronic, wrote about an experience he had with a dissenting director. George and all of the board, except this one person, were convinced that a particular acquisition should be made.[1] The dissenting director, however, was persistent in expressing his concerns in board discussions and in private conversations with George, who eventually became convinced the director was correct—the acquisition would be a mistake. He informed the rest of the board members, who then agreed the acquisition should not be made. Think about the personal fortitude such a stand required for the dissenting director, and think about how much he likely saved the company by sticking to his guns.

A good board both supports and challenges management—a very difficult balancing act that will require you to develop finely tuned orchestration skills. Encourage executives to express their opinions at board meetings and to react openly to directors' comments. But also encourage directors to listen well to executives and respect their ideas. The board must have exposure to the senior executive group both outside of formal board meetings as well as in them.

Recognize that you control most of the levers that will help directors grow their knowledge of the company. Meeting frequency and agenda management are crucial—it is your role to create the time needed for issues to be seriously discussed (not just "presented"). Ensure that there is an annual calendar of the main strategic issues that the board will discuss over the year and schedule these into meeting agendas. Allocate enough time for unrushed discussion of these matters, which may mean that some board meetings last a full day and sometimes longer. And be sure the board has the information it needs to understand the issues and contribute to the discussion.

Six to eight meetings a year that last only half a day each may not allow your board to engage seriously in the major issues facing the company. Conversely, if the board meets monthly, are you certain that this much time is really necessary? Is the "extra" time spent repeating the standard monthly agenda, or is it used to deal with different and more productive matters?

If you are the CEO, you must work hard to enable outside directors to understand how your company's business model works. Remember that it is difficult for part-time directors to grasp and retain all they really need to understand about your business. Don't be defensive when questioned, and don't think the independent directors are stupid or inattentive when they repeat their questions from one meeting to the next. They are periodically going to need help. Encourage open dialogue between your senior executives and the board. Crucially, don't forget that even the mildest board can turn feral if it feels it is being treated to too much "spin." Whether the news is good or bad, report it quickly and openly to the board.

If any of your executive colleagues are on the board as directors, remember, as we told them, that they are wearing a different hat when they sit at the board table. Make it clear to them that you understand this and that you want them to speak out. They aren't there to be your clones.

In many parts of the world, you may lead a company that has a large, controlling family shareholder, and your board may be widely seen as captive to that shareholder. Depending on where you are, governance standards—particularly the treatment of minority shareholders—may be the subject of a great deal of concern from other investors. This may hinder your company's efforts to tap global capital markets. How should you deal with this?

Many will tell you that you must appoint more independent directors to protect minority shareholders' interests. Your government might even be legislating or regulating in this direction, but you may still have a problem. Qualified and experienced independent directors can be in very short supply. In addition, many will assume—fairly or otherwise—that the independent directors on the board are still under the influence of the dominant family's interests.

As the leader of the board, you can have a major impact on how the other directors react to the various requirements and demands for improved corporate governance. On the one hand, you can decide on doing only what is necessary to "tick the boxes," or you can be serious about designing and leading a truly effective board. While you cannot and should not ignore external pressures for change, it is obviously our hope that you will focus on building the best board possible. Our approach to board design provides you with the tools to do this, but in the end, you and your fellow directors must put in the time and effort to accomplish this. As the board's leader, you must set the tone to make it happen.

Finally, regardless of whether you are the chairman only or both the chairman and CEO, and regardless of the jurisdiction in which you work, the key to your success as the board's leader is to build trust. Open dialogue is vital to your success. If we could offer only one piece of advice, it would be to strive for open communication among board members and between the board and management. This is the best guarantee of understanding and trust in the boardroom.

Leading the Independent Directors:
The Lead Director and the Committee Chairmen

A LONG WITH the chairman and CEO, you are all responsible for providing leadership to the board. Especially in situations where the chairman and CEO are the same person, you have a responsibility for leading the independent directors in meetings of the whole board and on committee work.

Your starting point is to clarify and agree on your duties with the chairman, the CEO, and the other directors. If you are the "lead director" or a committee chairman (in the United Kingdom you may be a "senior independent director"), develop a clear description of your duties. Putting them in writing is probably a good idea. Develop these in collaboration with your board colleagues. Without a clear definition, the expectations of the other directors, the chairman, and the CEO might be misplaced, making conflict between you and the board's other leaders possible. If you are the lead director, it is especially important that you have a clear agreement with the chairman/CEO about your duties, and that your board colleagues support this agreement.

As we pointed out in chapter 5, we believe the first responsibility of a lead director is to organize and moderate the meetings of non-executive directors. They should be scheduled as part of the board's routines so they will not cause undue angst for the CEO and his management team. While you should be ready to call a special meeting if it is needed, remember that you weren't appointed to create a "competing chairman" or to undermine his role. Your primary task is to facilitate a discussion among the independent directors to establish whether they have concerns about how the company and the board are being managed. Only in extreme circumstances, when the chairman and CEO cannot or should not be involved, are you expected to take charge.

You will, of course, provide feedback to the chairman/CEO on any issues or concerns raised in these meetings. Wherever possible, these issues should then be discussed between the CEO and the whole board. Again, open communication is what you should aim for. If you find yourself shuttling like an emissary between the chairman/ CEO and the other directors, something is seriously amiss. It's your job to figure out why and to create an open flow of communication.

Each board must also have a process to select leaders of the three major committees—audit, compensation, and corporate governance (nomination)—as well as any others. In the absence of an independent chairman, you, as leader of the independent directors, should partici- pate in these appointments as well as decisions assigning directors to the committees, or you should make sure that these decisions are being made through the corporate governance committee. Because these committees are expected to oversee management and ensure the inde- pendence of the board, it logically follows that you will need to be cer- tain that management is not unduly influencing those decisions. You have a responsibility to make sure that through their leadership and membership, these committees are truly independent.

Arguably, one of the board's most important tasks is the evaluation of the CEO. The independent directors will have to decide how this is to be done and who will lead the process. As we said in chapter 7, in too many boards, the CEO appraisal is done on the run as a postscript to the compensation committee's discussions about the money. As a result, many directors aren't involved in any meaningful discussion about the CEO's performance. The independent directors must agree among themselves about who takes the lead here—it could be you and/or the heads of the corporate governance or compensation com- mittees. It doesn't matter which of you, as long as there is clarity about who will take the lead. Then all the outside members of the board must be given an opportunity to participate in the process.

If you are a committee chairman, there are a few leadership issues you should think about. First, we urge that you avoid falling into the same trap as most committee chairs. They assume that as chairman, it's their obligation to do all the committee work. Rather than involv- ing other committee members, they do it all themselves. The other committee members show up at meetings and offer advice and opin- ions. The problem with this approach, especially as committees are being required to do more, is that the committee chairman becomes overwhelmed.

The solution? Expect and ask other members to take primary responsibility for some specific aspect of the committee's work. It will lighten your work as chairman, and it will also truly engage your fellow directors in the work of the committee.

A second issue you'll have to deal with is managing the relationship between your committee and the members of management who have expertise in the committee's domain, for example, financial executives and the audit committee; human resource executives and the compensation committee; and corporate counsel and corporate secretaries and the corporate governance committee. These managers clearly have knowledge and information that is critical to the committee's work. They should be invited to committee meetings to provide this information. However, it is your responsibility to see that their attendance does not compromise your committee's independence. It's a fine line to walk, but your committee must retain its independent perspective while gaining the necessary input from management.

Watch out also for the practice we've seen in many boards, where an executive who is supporting a committee writes a "script" to help the committee chairman give his report to the full board. We certainly believe that each committee should report its discussions as well as its requests for board action to the full board.[2] But these reports must reflect the independent directors' view of what transpired in the committee, not management's. Even an innocent attempt by management to be helpful can unintentionally compromise a committee's independence.

Finally, if you are chairman of one of the core committees, you will have to pay special heed to the increasing expectations that are being placed on your committee by changing rules and rising expectations of investors. It may seem that the requirements placed on your committee are going to be impossible to meet. We doubt it will become that difficult, but we do believe an essential part of your leadership job will be to determine how to meet these new expectations in the time available.

A Postscript: The Future of Boards

OUR TITLE—*Back to the Drawing Board*—is intended to empha-size that boards need to rethink their roles and practices—fine-tuning will not be enough. Board design in too many places is clearly flawed, and board practices are still captive to the traditions of a bygone era. It is time for a serious rethink.

Is the effort worthwhile? Some have argued that the public com-pany board has a limited future and will be eclipsed by other forms of direct equity investment that deliver superior performance, such as pri-vate equity and venture capital.[3] Certainly, these forms of investment and ownership have grown. Further, in many countries the majority of companies are owned by private capital, whether family controlled or by other groups.[4] Thus a significant part of the world economy is now governed by structures that don't conform to the public company model with the sorts of boards we have been discussing. But the pub-licly listed company is still a centrally important institution in modern economies. Further, venture capitalists, private equity investors, and other private companies also have boards of directors, although they can be very "hands on" and can drive performance improvement in ways that would often be viewed as unacceptable in a public company. Their board members aren't selected to avoid conflicts of interest; tidy distinctions between the roles of management and directors aren't observed (because directors often operate as quasi-executives). Such boards can challenge us to rethink the level of engagement that public company directors have in their companies.

Some have also argued that the notion of the "independent" board should be abandoned because it simply cannot work.[5] We don't agree. Yes, the board of a public company is an imperfect institution that struggles to measure up to investor and regulatory expectations. But no viable alternative has been proposed, so we must make the most of the best governance tools at our disposal. For now, that means inde-pendent boards. Our focus in this book is to enable them to perform their task better.

We have argued that the task of a board is very difficult. Unfortunately, the governance debate continues without a clear acknowledgement of that fact. Critics of board performance seem to believe that all that is required is for boards to wake up to their responsibilities, for the definitions of "independence" to be tightened, and for the proportion of independent directors to increase. We believe, however, that underestimating the difficulty of the task increases the risk of failure. Instead, we hope we have placed the real performance challenges faced by boards at the center of the governance debate.

We will be better off if we acknowledge that directors have inadequate time and a limited knowledge base to sufficiently meet their long list of responsibilities. Even if boards invest more time in their tasks, this problem will remain. Only if we recognize these facts will we be prompted to take all possible steps to address the problem. Thus, if yesterday and today's key themes in board governance are about "independence" and "alignment," tomorrow's key themes should be about better managing the tension between "time available" and "knowledge required." Board practice has been markedly influenced by the "independence and alignment" ideas. If similar energy is directed to addressing the challenges in using time and developing knowledge, we will see some genuine improvements inside our boardrooms in the coming decade.

Successful boards of the future will focus on *time* and *knowledge* as scarce resources, and work at ways to increase their own productivity. They will be more alert and knowledgeable about their companies for any given investment in time. Their leadership structures, the ways that new directors are selected, the ways that the board's work is organized and allocated among directors, and the ways that board and management relationships are nurtured—all of these will be designed to optimize the knowledge and understanding of directors, and the time available to the task. Each board will have to work out the answers that best suit its situation, finding creative ways to enhance its capacity to understand and engage meaningfully in its company. This will necessitate bold thinking and experimentation.

In this book we have outlined many ways that boards can do these things. We believe effective boards will be very different in the future—more differentiated in their roles, and more diverse and less dogma-driven in their design. Future boards will possess a genuine portfolio of diverse skills, accept more specialized roles among directors, and demonstrate a relationship of equals based on trust.

But we also know that their effectiveness will mostly be determined by the behavior of the people who sit on them. Governance activists and regulators are right to be concerned about structure and processes, and directors must heed their concerns. But all the rules in the world won't govern behavior behind closed doors in the boardroom. It's time to recognize the enormous burden that boards carry and understand that there is no universal "right" answer. The public company is still the engine of most economies, and boards have a crucial role in keeping that engine running. Directors cannot ignore external calls for change, but they must be wary of those that are so simplistic or punitive that our best business practitioners can't or won't accept seats. Directors need to think creatively to find the best-tailored solutions when they go back to the drawing board to design corporate boards that work effectively in the twenty-first century.

We understand that boards are far from perfect institutions. They are struggling and will likely continue to do so. What is needed is a concerted effort in many boardrooms and around the globe to improve this important institution. It is our hope that this book stimulates our readers to that end. To us, this is the best path forward for capitalism in all its forms.

Appendix: The Survey
of CEOs

In preparing this book, we surveyed CEOs of publicly listed companies to get their views about non-executive directors. We chose to approach CEOs because their opinions constitute a gap in the growing literature on boards. There have been many useful surveys of board structures and practices, as well as surveys to determine non-executive directors' views on a variety of issues pertaining to board practice and performance. Few, however, have sought to understand the CEO's perceptions and opinions.

CEOs' views are a crucial input to the corporate governance debate. These individuals play a critically important role in boards. They are a major influence on whether non-executive directors can do their jobs properly, and they occupy a privileged vantage point from which to observe non-executive directors at work.

Our challenge was to get behind the boardroom doors. We wanted to ask CEOs some tough questions about the effectiveness of their boards—including whether their directors understand their business, whether they work hard, and whether they remember things between meetings. We knew there was little prospect that CEOs would respond to a questionnaire, which was mailed to them, that asked questions of this type.

We decided to approach CEOs in person, through our own contacts but mostly through BCG partners around the world who approached the CEOs of client companies for us. Around 150 CEOs were approached in this way. They were told about the purpose of the survey and the work we were doing, then shown the questionnaire and asked if they would participate on the condition of anonymity. We received 132 responses from around the world, almost all from leading companies in their markets—from the S&P 500, FTSE 100, ASX 50, and the like—and including some of the largest and most prominent companies.

Needless to say, we are very grateful to the CEOs for their participation, and to our colleagues who approached them. Their views add an important and interesting dimension to the governance issues we discuss in this book, not only because of the role they occupy but also because they surprised us with some of the positions they advocated in the survey.

The survey was carried out in 2001, just before the corporate governance scandals and ensuing negative publicity. In that context, some of the responses are especially interesting to us. Even pre-Enron, for example, the CEOs believed that non-executive directors struggle, and the CEOs were also sceptical about the merits of risk-based compensation for boards.

We emphasize—and this is obvious—that our sample size is not large. Furthermore, the numbers of respondents by country are "lumpy" (we have, for example, more French than German CEOs). Nonetheless, we believe the results are interesting and enlightening. The consistency of responses was remarkable to us, and unexpected. On almost every issue, CEOs in every geography see the world in very similar ways. This gives us confidence in using the material here.

We should also point out that our 132 CEOs do not necessarily serve on 132 boards only. Many observe other boards as non-executive directors. In fact, they are likely to be commenting on a large pool of directors, probably somewhere between one thousand and two thousand strong.

The 132 responses are made up as follows

- North America 46 (United States 41, Canada 5)
- Europe 55 (United Kingdom 16, France 14, Spain 8, Germany 4, Sweden 4, Denmark 4, Netherlands 4, Switzerland 1)
- Asia Pacific 31 (Australia 15, Korea 8, India 4, Thailand 2, Hong Kong 1, Indonesia 1)

We did not include CEOs from Japan in the survey because there are, as yet, very few Japanese companies with outside directors. On the other hand, the largest Korean companies are now obliged to have outside directors on their boards and have several years of experience with what happens when "insider" boards make the transition to boards with "outsiders" in the majority.

What follows is the survey questionnaire and the results, which are reported in total and then by three regions (North America, Europe, and Asia Pacific), although in certain tables in the text, we have reported Asia and Australia (Asia Pacific) separately.

FIGURE A - 1

Proposition A-1: NEDs Must Understand What Drives Success in the Business

All CEO Responses (%)

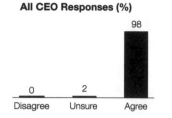

CEO Responses by Region (%)

Region	Disagree	Unsure	Agree
North America	0	2	98
Europe	0	4	96
Asia Pacific	0	0	100
Total	0	2	98

Note: The CEOs responded to a 5-point scale where 1 = Strongly Disagree to 5 = Strongly Agree. We have classified 1 and 2 as "disagree" and 4 and 5 as "agree." NED = Non-executive director.

Source: BCG HBS Global Survey of 132 CEOs in 2001 (Proposition A-1).

FIGURE A - 2

Proposition A-2: NEDs Must Do More than Ask Good Questions; They Must Be Sufficiently Informed to Contest Management's View

All CEO Responses (%)

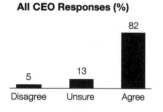

CEO Responses by Region (%)

Region	Disagree	Unsure	Agree
North America	2	22	76
Europe	7	9	84
Asia Pacific	3	7	90
Total	5	13	82

Note: The CEOs responded to a 5-point scale where 1 = Strongly Disagree to 5 = Strongly Agree. We have classified 1 and 2 as "disagree" and 4 and 5 as "agree." NED = Non-executive director.

Source: BCG HBS Global Survey of 132 CEOs in 2001 (Proposition A-2).

FIGURE A - 3

Proposition A-3: In Multibusiness Companies, NEDs Must Understand the Major Strategy Issues in Each of the Major Businesses

All CEO Responses (%)

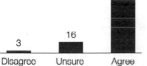

Disagree   Unsure   Agree

CEO Responses by Region (%)

Region	Disagree	Unsure	Agree
North America	2	22	76
Europe	4	18	78
Asia Pacific	3	3	94
Total	3	16	81

Note: The CEOs responded to a 5-point scale where 1 = Strongly Disagree to 5 = Strongly Agree.
We have classified 1 and 2 as "disagree" and 4 and 5 as "agree."
NED = Non-executive director.

Source: BCG HBS Global Survey of 132 CEOs in 2001 (Proposition A-3).

FIGURE A - 4

Proposition A-4: NEDs Must Be Sufficiently Informed to Make Decisions on Major Strategic Moves

All CEO Responses (%)

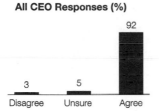

Disagree   Unsure   Agree

CEO Responses by Region (%)

Region	Disagree	Unsure	Agree
North America	0	4	96
Europe	4	4	92
Asia Pacific	7	7	86
Total	3	5	92

Note: The CEOs responded to a 5-point scale where 1 = Strongly Disagree to 5 = Strongly Agree.
We have classified 1 and 2 as "disagree" and 4 and 5 as "agree."
NED = Non-executive director.

Source: BCG HBS Global Survey of 132 CEOs in 2001 (Proposition A-4).

FIGURE A - 5

Proposition A-5: NEDs Must Know the Qualities of the Executives Who Are Candidates for the Most Senior Positions in the Company

All CEO Responses (%)

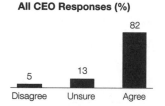

CEO Responses by Region (%)

Region	Disagree	Unsure	Agree
North America	2	0	98
Europe	5	24	71
Asia Pacific	10	13	77
Total	5	13	82

Note: The CEOs responded to a 5-point scale where 1 = Strongly Disagree to 5 = Strongly Agree.
     We have classified 1 and 2 as "disagree" and 4 and 5 as "agree."
     NED = Non-executive director.

Source: BCG HBS Global Survey of 132 CEOs in 2001 (Proposition A-5).

FIGURE A - 6

Proposition B-1: NEDs Do Understand the Factors That Drive Performance in Each of the Main Businesses

All CEO Responses (%)

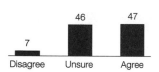

CEO Responses by Region (%)

Region	Disagree	Unsure	Agree
North America	4	50	46
Europe	9	42	49
Asia Pacific	7	47	46
Total	7	46	47

Note: The CEOs responded to a 5-point scale where 1 = Strongly Disagree to 5 = Strongly Agree.
     We have classified 1 and 2 as "disagree" and 4 and 5 as "agree."
     NED = Non-executive director.

Source: BCG HBS Global Survey of 132 CEOs in 2001 (Proposition B-1).

FIGURE A - 7

Proposition B-2: NEDs Are Well Prepared for Board Meetings

All CEO Responses (%)

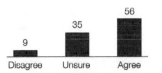

Disagree	Unsure	Agree

CEO Responses by Region (%)

Region	Disagree	Unsure	Agree
North America	2	41	57
Europe	11	36	53
Asia Pacific	17	23	60
Total	9	35	56

Note: The CEOs responded to a 5-point scale where 1 = Strongly Disagree to 5 = Strongly Agree. We have classified 1 and 2 as "disagree" and 4 and 5 as "agree." NED = Non-executive director.

Source: BCG HBS Global Survey of 132 CEOs in 2001 (Proposition B-2).

FIGURE A - 8

Proposition B-3: NEDs Recall Previous Discussions, and Management Doesn't Have to Keep Repeating Things in Subsequent Meetings

All CEO Responses (%)

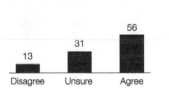

Disagree	Unsure	Agree

CEO Responses by Region (%)

Region	Disagree	Unsure	Agree
North America	20	28	52
Europe	9	31	60
Asia Pacific	10	37	53
Total	13	31	56

Note: The CEOs responded to a 5-point scale where 1 = Strongly Disagree to 5 = Strongly Agree. We have classified 1 and 2 as "disagree" and 4 and 5 as "agree." NED = Non-executive director.

Source: BCG HBS Global Survey of 132 CEOs in 2001 (Proposition B-3).

FIGURE A - 9

Proposition B-4: NEDs Often Raise Important New Issues in Board Discussions

All CEO Responses (%)

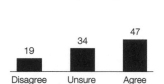

Disagree   Unsure   Agree

CEO Responses by Region (%)

Region	Disagree	Unsure	Agree
North America	11	24	65
Europe	24	40	36
Asia Pacific	23	37	40
Total	19	34	47

Note: The CEOs responded to a 5-point scale where 1 = Strongly Disagree to 5 = Strongly Agree. We have classified 1 and 2 as "disagree" and 4 and 5 as "agree." NED = Non-executive director.

Source: BCG HBS Global Survey of 132 CEOs in 2001 (Proposition B-4).

FIGURE A - 10

Proposition B-5: NEDs Accept Accountability for Their Role in Major Decisions

All CEO Responses (%)

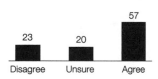

Disagree   Unsure   Agree

CEO Responses by Region (%)

Region	Disagree	Unsure	Agree
North America	21	12	67
Europe	20	25	55
Asia Pacific	30	20	50
Total	23	20	57

Note: The CEOs responded to a 5-point scale where 1 = Strongly Disagree to 5 = Strongly Agree. We have classified 1 and 2 as "disagree" and 4 and 5 as "agree." NED = Non-executive director.

Source: BCG HBS Global Survey of 132 CEOs in 2001 (Proposition B-5).

FIGURE A - 11

Proposition B-6: NEDs Spend Enough Time with Management to Be Able to Judge Management Succession Issues

All CEO Responses (%)

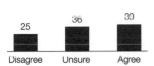

Disagree	Unsure	Agree
25	36	30

CEO Responses by Region (%)

Region	Disagree	Unsure	Agree
North America	13	24	63
Europe	33	47	20
Asia Pacific	32	34	34
Total	25	36	39

Note: The CEOs responded to a 5-point scale where 1 = Strongly Disagree to 5 = Strongly Agree.
We have classified 1 and 2 as "disagree" and 4 and 5 as "agree."
NED = Non-executive director.

Source: BCG HBS Global Survey of 132 CEOs in 2001 (Proposition B-6).

FIGURE A - 12

Proposition B-7: NEDs Focus on the Important Issues at Board Meetings

All CEO Responses (%)

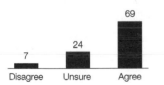

Disagree	Unsure	Agree
7	24	69

CEO Responses by Region (%)

Region	Disagree	Unsure	Agree
North America	4	33	63
Europe	7	17	76
Asia Pacific	10	27	63
Total	7	24	69

Note: The CEOs responded to a 5-point scale where 1 = Strongly Disagree to 5 = Strongly Agree.
We have classified 1 and 2 as "disagree" and 4 and 5 as "agree."
NED = Non-executive director.

Source: BCG HBS Global Survey of 132 CEOs in 2001 (Proposition B-7).

FIGURE A - 13

Proposition B-8: NEDs' Contribution Is Constructive in Tone and Made in a Way That Is Supportive of Management

All CEO Responses (%)

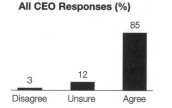

CEO Responses by Region (%)

Region	Disagree	Unsure	Agree
North America	0	11	89
Europe	4	9	87
Asia Pacific	7	20	73
Total	3	12	85

Note: The CEOs responded to a 5-point scale where 1 = Strongly Disagree to 5 = Strongly Agree. We have classified 1 and 2 as "disagree" and 4 and 5 as "agree." NED = Non-executive director.

Source: BCG HBS Global Survey of 132 CEOs in 2001 (Proposition B-8).

FIGURE A - 14

Proposition B-9: Board Discussions Conclude with Clear Direction to Management

All CEO Responses (%)

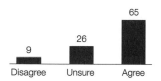

CEO Responses by Region (%)

Region	Disagree	Unsure	Agree
North America	11	30	59
Europe	11	27	62
Asia Pacific	3	17	80
Total	9	26	65

Note: The CEOs responded to a 5-point scale where 1 = Strongly Disagree to 5 = Strongly Agree. We have classified 1 and 2 as "disagree" and 4 and 5 as "agree." NED = Non-executive director.

Source: BCG HBS Global Survey of 132 CEOs in 2001 (Proposition B-9).

FIGURE A - 15

Proposition B-10: Periodically, NEDs Review Whether Agreed-upon Initiatives Have Been Implemented

All CEO Responses (%)

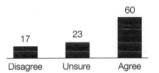

Disagree 17   Unsure 23   Agree 60

CEO Responses by Region (%)

Region	Disagree	Unsure	Agree
North America	17	22	61
Europe	18	20	62
Asia Pacific	13	30	57
Total	17	23	60

Note: The CEOs responded to a 5-point scale where 1 = Strongly Disagree to 5 = Strongly Agree.
We have classified 1 and 2 as "disagree" and 4 and 5 as "agree."
NED = Non-executive director.

Source: BCG HBS Global Survey of 132 CEOs in 2001 (Proposition B-10).

FIGURE A - 16

Proposition C-1: NEDs Must Spend More Time on the Job Learning About the Business and Its People As Well As the Industries in Which We Operate

All CEO Responses (%)

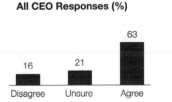

Disagree 16   Unsure 21   Agree 63

CEO Responses by Region (%)

Region	Disagree	Unsure	Agree
North America	18	25	57
Europe	13	20	67
Asia Pacific	20	17	63
Total	16	21	63

Note: The CEOs responded to a 5-point scale where 1 = Strongly Disagree to 5 = Strongly Agree.
We have classified 1 and 2 as "disagree" and 4 and 5 as "agree."
NED = Non-executive director.

Source: BCG HBS Global Survey of 132 CEOs in 2001 (Proposition C-1).

Proposition C-2: To Cope with Complexity, NEDs Will Have to Allocate Some of the Issues Among Themselves Rather than Try to Cover Everything

All CEO Responses (%)

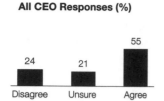

Disagree   Unsure   Agree

CEO Responses by Region (%)

Region	Disagree	Unsure	Agree
North America	24	20	56
Europe	29	24	47
Asia Pacific	17	17	66
Total	24	21	55

Note: The CEOs responded to a 5-point scale where 1 = Strongly Disagree to 5 = Strongly Agree. We have classified 1 and 2 as "disagree" and 4 and 5 as "agree." NED = Non-executive director.

Source: BCG HBS Global Survey of 132 CEOs in 2001 (Proposition C-2).

Proposition C-3: NEDs Will Spend More Time Outside Board Meetings Learning About the Business with Employees, Customers, and Suppliers

All CEO Responses (%)

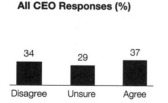

Disagree   Unsure   Agree

CEO Responses by Region (%)

Region	Disagree	Unsure	Agree
North America	41	24	35
Europe	34	24	42
Asia Pacific	21	48	31
Total	34	29	37

Note: The CEOs responded to a 5-point scale where 1 = Strongly Disagree to 5 = Strongly Agree. We have classified 1 and 2 as "disagree" and 4 and 5 as "agree." NED = Non-executive director.

Source: BCG HBS Global Survey of 132 CEOs in 2001 (Proposition C-3).

FIGURE A - 19

Proposition C-4: Performance Evaluation Will Need to Strengthen and Low-Performing Directors Moved Out

All CEO Responses (%)

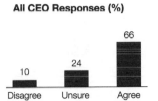

	Disagree	Unsure	Agree
	10	24	66

CEO Responses by Region (%)

Region	Disagree	Unsure	Agree
North America	15	30	55
Europe	9	25	66
Asia Pacific	3	13	84
Total	10	24	66

Note: The CEOs responded to a 5-point scale where 1 = Strongly Disagree to 5 = Strongly Agree.
We have classified 1 and 2 as "disagree" and 4 and 5 as "agree."
NED = Non-executive director.

Source: BCG HBS Global Survey of 132 CEOs in 2001 (Proposition C-4).

FIGURE A - 20

Proposition C-5: Outside Directors Should Be Required to Own Stock in the Business in Amounts That Are Very Material to Them

All CEO Responses (%)

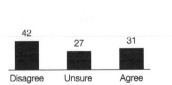

	Disagree	Unsure	Agree
	42	27	31

CEO Responses by Region (%)

Region	Disagree	Unsure	Agree
North America	35	26	39
Europe	56	24	20
Asia Pacific	32	34	34
Total	42	27	31

Note: The CEOs responded to a 5-point scale where 1 = Strongly Disagree to 5 = Strongly Agree.
We have classified 1 and 2 as "disagree" and 4 and 5 as "agree."
NED = Non-executive director.

Source: BCG HBS Global Survey of 132 CEOs in 2001 (Proposition C-5).

FIGURE A- 21

Proposition C-6: Remuneration of Outside Directors Should Substantially Be at Risk—Being Paid in Stock and Options

All CEO Responses (%)

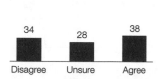

Disagree	Unsure	Agree
34	28	38

CEO Responses by Region (%)

Region	Disagree	Unsure	Agree
North America	13	35	52
Europe	49	25	26
Asia Pacific	37	23	40
Total	34	28	38

Note: The CEOs responded to a 5-point scale where 1 = Strongly Disagree to 5 = Strongly Agree. We have classified 1 and 2 as "disagree" and 4 and 5 as "agree." NED = Non-executive director.

Source: BCG HBS Global Survey of 132 CEOs in 2001 (Proposition C-6).

FIGURE A - 22

Proposition C-7: The Scope of the Board's Role and Accountability Will Have to Be Narrowed in Order for It to Be More Effective

All CEO Responses (%)

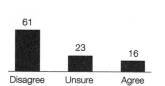

Disagree	Unsure	Agree
61	23	16

CEO Responses by Region (%)

Region	Disagree	Unsure	Agree
North America	70	20	10
Europe	56	27	17
Asia Pacific	57	20	23
Total	61	23	16

Note: The CEOs responded to a 5-point scale where 1 = Strongly Disagree to 5 = Strongly Agree. We have classified 1 and 2 as "disagree" and 4 and 5 as "agree." NED = Non-executive director.

Source: BCG HBS Global Survey of 132 CEOs in 2001 (Proposition C-7).

FIGURE A - 23

Proposition C-8: In the Future, Boards Will Have to Increase Their Focus on the Interests of All Stakeholders, Not Only the Shareholders

All CEO Responses (%)

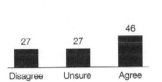

Disagree	Unsure	Agree
27	27	46

CEO Responses by Region (%)

Region	Disagree	Unsure	Agree
North America	26	30	44
Europe	36	27	37
Asia Pacific	13	20	67
Total	27	27	46

Note: The CEOs responded to a 5-point scale where 1 = Strongly Disagree to 5 = Strongly Agree. We have classified 1 and 2 as "disagree" and 4 and 5 as "agree." NED = Non-executive director.

Source: BCG HBS Global Survey of 132 CEOs in 2001 (Proposition C-8).

FIGURE A - 24

Proposition C-9: Boards Need Directors from More Diverse Backgrounds

All CEO Responses (%)

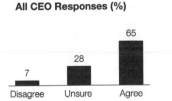

Disagree	Unsure	Agree
7	28	65

CEO Responses by Region (%)

Region	Disagree	Unsure	Agree
North America	7	31	62
Europe	5	33	62
Asia Pacific	10	14	76
Total	7	28	65

Note: The CEOs responded to a 5-point scale where 1 = Strongly Disagree to 5 = Strongly Agree. We have classified 1 and 2 as "disagree" and 4 and 5 as "agree." NED = Non-executive director.

Source: BCG HBS Global Survey of 132 CEOs in 2001 (Proposition C-9).

FIGURE A - 25

Proposition D-1: Boards Are Increasingly Involved in the Oversight of Their Companies

All CEO Responses (%)

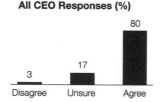

CEO Responses by Region (%)

Region	Disagree	Unsure	Agree
North America	2	17	81
Europe	0	13	87
Asia Pacific	7	27	66
Total	3	17	80

Note: The CEOs responded to a 5-point scale where 1 = Strongly Disagree to 5 = Strongly Agree. We have classified 1 and 2 as "disagree" and 4 and 5 as "agree." NED = Non-executive director.

Source: BCG HBS Global Survey of 132 CEOs in 2001 (Proposition D-1).

FIGURE A - 26

Proposition D-2: Boards Are Increasingly Effective in Discharging Their Duties

All CEO Responses (%)

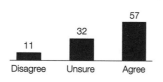

CEO Responses by Region (%)

Region	Disagree	Unsure	Agree
North America	9	30	61
Europe	11	40	49
Asia Pacific	17	20	63
Total	11	32	57

Note: The CEOs responded to a 5-point scale where 1 = Strongly Disagree to 5 = Strongly Agree. We have classified 1 and 2 as "disagree" and 4 and 5 as "agree." NED = Non-executive director.

Source: BCG HBS Global Survey of 132 CEOs in 2001 (Proposition D-2).

FIGURE A - 27

Proposition E-1: CEOs or Ex-CEOs Make the Best Directors

All CEO Responses (%)

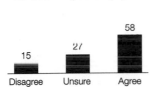

| Disagree | Unsure | Agree |

CEO Responses by Region (%)

Region	Disagree	Unsure	Agree
North America	20	17	63
Europe	15	36	49
Asia Pacific	7	26	67
Total	15	27	58

Note: The CEOs responded to a 5-point scale where 1 = Strongly Disagree to 5 = Strongly Agree.
We have classified 1 and 2 as "disagree" and 4 and 5 as "agree."
NED = Non-executive director.

Source: BCG HBS Global Survey of 132 CEOs in 2001 (Proposition E-1).

FIGURE A - 28

Proposition E-2: Except for the CEO, All Directors on a Board Should Be Independent

All CEO Responses (%)

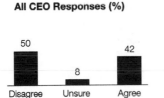

| Disagree | Unsure | Agree |

CEO Responses by Region (%)

Region	Disagree	Unsure	Agree
North America	42	4	54
Europe	59	11	30
Asia Pacific	47	10	43
Total	50	8	42

Note: The CEOs responded to a 5-point scale where 1 = Strongly Disagree to 5 = Strongly Agree.
We have classified 1 and 2 as "disagree" and 4 and 5 as "agree."
NED = Non-executive director.

Source: BCG HBS Global Survey of 132 CEOs in 2001 (Proposition E-2).

Proposition E-3: Smaller Boards With, Say, Ten or Fewer Members, Are More Effective

All CEO Responses (%)

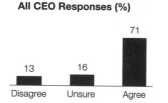

| | Disagree | Unsure | Agree |
| 13 | 16 | 71 |

CEO Responses by Region (%)

Region	Disagree	Unsure	Agree
North America	24	17	59
Europe	7	21	72
Asia Pacific	7	3	90
Total	13	16	71

Note: The CEOs responded to a 5-point scale where 1 = Strongly Disagree to 5 = Strongly Agree. We have classified 1 and 2 as "disagree" and 4 and 5 as "agree." NED = Non-executive director.

Source: BCG HBS Global Survey of 132 CEOs in 2001 (Proposition E-3).

Proposition E-4: Independent Directors Struggle to Understand the Business

All CEO Responses (%)

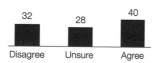

| | Disagree | Unsure | Agree |
| 32 | 28 | 40 |

CEO Responses by Region (%)

Region	Disagree	Unsure	Agree
North America	41	26	33
Europe	25	31	44
Asia Pacific	31	28	41
Total	32	28	40

Note: The CEOs responded to a 5-point scale where 1 = Strongly Disagree to 5 = Strongly Agree. We have classified 1 and 2 as "disagree" and 4 and 5 as "agree." NED = Non-executive director.

Source: BCG HBS Global Survey of 132 CEOs in 2001 (Proposition E-4).

FIGURE A - 31

Proposition E-5: Replacing Poorly Performing Directors Is Very Difficult

All CEO Responses (%)

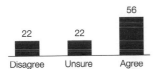

Disagree	22
Unsure	22
Agree	56

CEO Responses by Region (%)

Region	Disagree	Unsure	Agree
North America	11	15	74
Europe	33	28	39
Asia Pacific	17	24	59
Total	22	22	56

Note: The CEOs responded to a 5-point scale where 1 = Strongly Disagree to 5 = Strongly Agree.
We have classified 1 and 2 as "disagree" and 4 and 5 as "agree."
NED = Non-executive director.

Source: BCG HBS Global Survey of 132 CEOs in 2001 (Proposition E-5).

FIGURE A - 32

Proposition E-6: A Board Can Only Be Effective if the CEO Wants It to Be Effective

All CEO Responses (%)

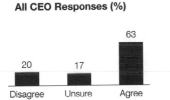

Disagree	20
Unsure	17
Agree	63

CEO Responses by Region (%)

Region	Disagree	Unsure	Agree
North America	15	11	74
Europe	22	22	56
Asia Pacific	23	17	60
Total	20	17	63

Note: The CEOs responded to a 5-point scale where 1 = Strongly Disagree to 5 = Strongly Agree.
We have classified 1 and 2 as "disagree" and 4 and 5 as "agree."
NED = Non-executive director.

Source: BCG HBS Global Survey of 132 CEOs in 2001 (Proposition E-6).

Proposition E-7: All Boards Should Have Strong Independent Leadership—Either a Separate Non-Executive Chairman or a Designated Lead Director

All CEO Responses (%)

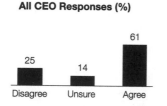

CEO Responses by Region (%)

Region	Disagree	Unsure	Agree
North America	47	11	42
Europe	17	18	65
Asia Pacific	10	10	80
Total	25	14	61

Note: The CEOs responded to a 5-point scale where 1 = Strongly Disagree to 5 = Strongly Agree. We have classified 1 and 2 as "disagree" and 4 and 5 as "agree." NED = Non-executive director.

Source: BCG HBS Global Survey of 132 CEOs in 2001 (Proposition E-7).

Proposition E-8: The Governance Debate Is Too Much About "Ticking Boxes." What Really Counts Are Skills and Behaviors Inside the Boardroom.

All CEO Responses (%)

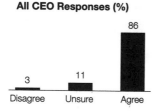

CEO Responses by Region (%)

Region	Disagree	Unsure	Agree
North America	7	16	77
Europe	2	13	85
Asia Pacific	0	0	100
Total	3	11	86

Note: The CEOs responded to a 5-point scale where 1 = Strongly Disagree to 5 = Strongly Agree. We have classified 1 and 2 as "disagree" and 4 and 5 as "agree." NED = Non-executive director.

Source: BCG HBS Global Survey of 132 CEOs in 2001 (Proposition E-8).

Notes

Chapter One

1. Sarbanes-Oxley Act of 2002, Public Law 107-204, 107th Congress, enacted 30 July 2002 (the "Sarbanes-Oxley Act"), available at <http://news.findlaw.com/hdocs/docs/gwbush/sarbanesoxley072302.pdf> (accessed 13 May 2003).

2. New York Stock Exchange, "Corporate Governance Rule Proposals," 1 August 2002, available at <http://www.nyse.com/pdfs/corp_gov_pro_b.pdf> (accessed 16 May 2003), as amended by Amendment No. 1, 4 April 2003, available at <http://www.nyse.com/pdfs/amend1-04-09-03.pdf> (accessed 16 May 2003); NASDAQ, "Summary of NASDAQ Corporate Governance Proposals," 26 February 2003, available at <http://www.nasdaq.com/about/Web_Corp_Gov_Summary%20Feb-revised.pdf> (accessed 16 May 2003); American Stock Exchange, "Enhanced Corporate Governance—Text of Proposed Rule Changes," 16 May 2003, available at <http://www.amex.com> (accessed 16 May 2003). Note that approval of these proposed rules by the Securities and Exchange Commission were pending as of May 2003.

3. The Committee on the Financial Aspects of Corporate Governance, *Report of the Committee on the Financial Aspects of Corporate Governance* (the "Cadbury Report") (London: Gee and Co. Ltd., 1992). In honor of the committee's chair, it is popularly known as the "Cadbury Report."

4. Derek Higgs, *Review of the Role and Effectiveness of Non-Executive Directors* (the "Higgs Report") (London: Department of Trade and Industry, 2003); and Sir Robert Smith, *Audit Committees Combined Code Guidance* (the "Smith Report") (London: Financial Reporting Council, 2003). In each case, the report is popularly named after the committee's chair.

5. General Motors Board of Directors, *GM Board Guidelines on Significant Corporate Governance Issues* (New York: General Motors, 1994).

6. See Jay W. Lorsch, Rakesh Khurana, and Sonya U. Sanchez, "Delphi Corporation," Case N4-402-033 (Boston: Harvard Business School, forthcoming).

7. Excerpts from Thomas H. Wyman's remarks at the National Association of Corporate Directors Annual Conference in April 2002 were published in Thomas H. Wyman, "Directorship: Lessons from Delphi," *Director's Monthly*, July 2002, 8–10.

8. In partnership with the Organisation for Economic Co-operation and Development (OECD), the World Bank sponsors the Global Corporate Governance Forum, which aims to assist transition economies in improving the quality of their corporate governance. James Wolfensohn, the president of the World Bank, has remarked that "The governance of the corporation is now as important in the world economy as the government of countries" (see Global Corporate Governance Forum Web site at <http://www.gcgf.org/about.htm> (accessed 13 May 2003)). See also Magdi R. Iskander and Nadereh Chamlou, *Corporate Governance: A Framework for Implementation* (Washington, DC: The World Bank Group, 2000). In 1999, the OECD published its own corporate governance principles. Ad Hoc Task Force on Corporate Governance, *OECD Principles of Corporate Governance* (Paris: Organisation for Economic Co-Operation and Development, 1999). And in responding to financial crises in recent years, the International Monetary Fund (IMF) has also taken an active interest in corporate governance. As one Council on Foreign Relations study put it, "Reform of corporate governance was at the heart of the comprehensive reform package put together during the Asian crisis by [the IMF], especially with regard to Korea." In addition to pushing Korean business groups to reduce debt and focus on core businesses, the IMF "demanded that Korea institute a governance system whereby the power of minority shareholders and outside directors would be vastly enhanced." Meredith Woo-Cumings, "Economic Crisis and Corporate Reform in East Asia," *A Paper from the Project on Development, Trade, and International Finance* (New York: The Council on Foreign Relations, 2000).

9. Committee on Corporate Governance, *Corporate Governance in the Netherlands: Forty Recommendations* (the "Peters Report") (Amsterdam: Committee on Corporate Governance, 1997), <http://www.ecgi.org/codes/country_documents/netherlands/nl-peters_report.pdf> (accessed 11 May 2003). It is popularly known as the "Peters Report" in honor of the committee chair.

10. Conseil National du Patronat Français & Association Française des Entreprises Privées, "The Boards of Directors of Listed Companies in France," 10 July 1995, available at <http://www.ecgi.org/codes/country_documents/france/vienot1_en.pdf> (accessed 11 May 2003); Association Française des Entreprises Privées & Mouvement des Entreprises de France, "Report of the Committee on Corporate Governance," July 1999, <http://www.ecgi.org/codes/country_documents/france/vienot2_en.pdf> (accessed 11 May 2003); and Mouvement des Entreprises de France & Association Française des Entreprises Privées, "Promoting Better Corporate Governance in Listed Companies," 23 September 2002, <http://www.ecgi.org/codes/country_documents/france/rapport_bouton_en.pdf> (accessed 11 May 2003). These are commonly referred to, respectively, as the "Vienot I," "Vienot II," and "Bouton" Reports, in honor of the committee chairmen.

11. Government Commission, "German Corporate Governance Code," 26 February 2002, available at <http://www.ecgi.org/codes/country_documents/germany/corgov_

endfassung_e.pdf> (accessed 11 May 2003). This best practice code is commonly known as the "Cromme Code" in honor of the committee chairman.

12. The Australian government's proposals for dealing with corporate disclosure were published in Corporate Disclosure: Strengthening the Financial Reporting Framework, CLERP Paper No. 9 (September 2002). The independence of auditors was addressed in Independence of *Australian Company Auditors: Review of Current Australian Requirements and Proposals for Reform—Report to the Minister for Financial Services and Regulation* (October 2001). This report is known as the Ramsay Report after its author, Professor Ian Ramsay. The Australian Stock Exchange (ASX) issued its governance guidelines, *The Corporate Governance Council: Principles of Good Governance and Best Practice Recommendations* (March 2003).

13. Committee on Corporate Governance, "Code of Best Practice for Corporate Governance," September 1999, available at <http://www.ecgi.org/codes/country_documents/korea/code_korea.pdf> (accessed 11 May 2003). Recent Korean corporate governance reform legislation is described in Bernard Black, Barry Metzger, Timothy O'Brien, and Young Moo Shin, "Corporate Governance in Korea at the Millennium: Enhancing International Competitiveness—Final Report and Legal Reform Recommendations to the Ministry of Justice of the Republic of Korea 15 May 2000," *Journal of Corporation Law* 26, no. 3 (2001): 537–608.

14. See, for example, Japan Corporate Governance Committee, "Revised Corporate Governance Principles," 26 October 2001, available at <http://www.ecgi.org/codes/country_documents/japan/revised_corporate_governance_principles.pdf> (accessed 11 May 2003).

Chapter Two

1. Rakesh Khurana, *Searching for a Corporate Savior: The Irrational Quest for Charismatic CEOs* (Princeton, NJ: Princeton University Press, 2002), 59–60.

2. The Sarbanes-Oxley Act requires that every member of the audit committee meet stringent criteria for independence; and that the audit committee be directly responsible for appointing, compensating, and overseeing the company's outside auditor. Sarbanes-Oxley Act of 2002, Public Law 107-204, 107th Congress, enacted 30 July 2002 (the "Sarbanes-Oxley Act"), available at <http://news.findlaw.com/hdocs/docs/gwbush/sarbanesoxley072302.pdf> (accessed 13 May 2003), sec. 301. The Smith Report similarly calls for the audit committee to be made up of independent directors and expands the committee's responsibilities, but leaves the appointment of the outside auditor to the full board (with the audit committee making a recommendation). Sir Robert Smith, *Audit Committees Combined Code Guidance* (the "Smith Report") (London: Financial Reporting Council, 2003), para. 2.1.

3. Only very large and complex U.S. companies meet once a month, including the very largest companies such as Ford, General Electric, and General Motors.

4. Egon Zehnder International, *Board of Directors Global Study* (London: Egon Zehnder International, 2000), 40, 52. Another search firm found a higher average for directors of large U.S. companies—156 hours per year in its 2001 survey, and 183 hours in its 2002 survey, but these figures included travel time to meetings. See Korn/Ferry

International, *28th Annual Board of Directors Study 2001* (Los Angeles: Korn/Ferry International, 2001), 18; and Korn/Ferry International, *29th Annual Board of Directors Study 2002: Fortune 1000 Highlights* (Los Angeles: Korn/Ferry International, 2002), 14.

5. Egon Zehnder International, *Board of Directors Global Study,* 56–57.

6. In Germany, supervisory boards in larger companies often have twenty members, as required by law.

7. For example, two books that said little about independent directors' time and knowledge *constraints* while calling for boards to play a more substantial role in strategy are Ram Charan, *Boards at Work: How Corporate Boards Create Competitive Advantage* (San Francisco: Jossey-Bass, 1998); and Susan Shultz, *The Board Book: Making Your Corporate Board a Strategic Force in Your Company's Success* (New York: Amacom, 2001).

8. Recent books emphasizing the extraordinary pace of change and complexity with which today's companies have to deal include Nitin Nohria, Davis Dyer, and Frederick Dalzell, *Changing Fortunes: Remaking the Industrial Corporation* (New York: Wiley, 2002); Richard N. Foster and Sarah Kaplan, *Creative Destruction* (New York: Doubleday, 2001); Chris Zook and James Allen, *Profit from the Core: Growth Strategy in an Era of Turbulence* (Boston: Harvard Business School Press, 2001); Gary Hamel, *Leading the Revolution* (Boston: Harvard Business School Press, 2000); and Donald C. Hambrick, David A. Nadler, and Michael L. Tushman, *Navigating Change* (Boston: Harvard Business School Press, 1998).

9. Egon Zehnder International, *Board of Directors Global Study,* 21.

10. Marconi, which had a market capitalization of 35 billion pounds sterling at its peak in 2000, lost more than 99 percent of its value in less than two years. See Dominic White, "Decline and Fall of Weinstock's Mighty Empire," *The Daily Telegraph,* 29 August 2002, 33.

11. The intellectual source of this view rests in a seminal article: Michael C. Jensen and William H. Meckling, "Theory of the Firm: Managerial Behavior, Agency Costs and Ownership Structure," *Journal of Financial Economics* 3, no. 4 (1976): 305–360.

12. See Frederick F. Reichheld, *The Loyalty Effect* (Boston: Harvard Business School Press, 1996).

13. See Peter F. Drucker, "Knowledge-Worker Productivity: The Biggest Challenge," *California Management Review,* Winter 1999, 79–94.

14. For an exploration of this issue, see Felix Barber, Jeff Kotzen, Eric Olsen, and Rainer Strack, "Quantifying Employee Contribution," *Shareholder Value,* May/June 2002, 52–58.

15. In the United States, these include, among others, the Sarbanes-Oxley Act; the various rule changes proposed by the stock exchanges, see New York Stock Exchange, "Corporate Governance Rule Proposals," 1 August 2002, available at <http://www.nyse.com/pdfs/corp_gov_pro_b.pdf> (accessed 16 May 2003), as amended by Amendment No. 1, 4 April 2003, available at <http://www.nyse.com/pdfs/amend 1-04-09-03.pdf> (accessed 16 May 2003); NASDAQ, "Summary of NASDAQ Corporate Governance Proposals," 26 February 2003, available at <http://www.nasdaq.com/about/Web_Corp_Gov_Summary%20Feb-revised.pdf> (accessed 16 May 2003); American Stock Exchange, "Enhanced Corporate Governance—Text of Proposed Rule

Changes," 16 May 2003, available at <http://www.amex.com> (accessed 16 May 2003); and the Conference Board Commission on Public Trust and Private Enterprise, *Corporate Governance: Principles, Recommendations and Specific Best Practice Suggestions* (New York: The Conference Board, 2003). In the United Kingdom, the most recent proposals for change are the Higgs Report on non-executive directors and boards more generally, see Derek Higgs, *Review of the Role and Effectiveness of Non-Executive Directors* (the "Higgs Report") (London: Department of Trade and Industry, 2003); and the Smith Report on audit committees.

16. See, for example, Ira M. Millstein and Paul W. MacAvoy, "The Active Board of Directors and Performance of the Large Publicly Traded Corporation," *Columbia Law Review* 98 (1998): 1283–1322; and Paul A. Gompers, Joy L. Ishii, and Andrew Metrick, "Corporate Governance and Equity Prices," *Quarterly Journal of Economics* 18, no. 1 (2003): 107–155. But note that neither of these studies purported to have found a *causal* relationship between externally observable aspects of boards and company financial performance.

17. Egon Zehnder International, *Board of Directors Global Study*, 52.

Chapter Three

1. What proportion of the board should be independent varies from country to country. For example, in the United States and Australia, the ideal is to have only one or two management directors, while in the United Kingdom the ideal seems to be that about half the board should be independent.

2. Ensuring the genuine independence of these non-executive directors is a principal theme of the stock exchanges' proposed rule revisions; see, for example, New York Stock Exchange, "Corporate Governance Rule Proposals," 1 August 2002, available at <http://www.nyse.com/pdfs/corp_gov_pro_b.pdf> (accessed 16 May 2003), as amended by Amendment No. 1, 4 April 2003, available at <http://www.nyse.com/pdfs/amend1-04-09-03.pdf> (accessed 16 May 2003), subsec. 1 and 2. This is also an important objective of the Sarbanes-Oxley Act in regard to audit committee members, Sarbanes-Oxley Act of 2002, Public Law 107-204, 107th Congress, enacted 30 July 2002 (the "Sarbanes-Oxley Act"), available at <http://news.findlaw.com/hdocs/docs/gwbush/sarbanesoxley072302.pdf> (accessed 13 May 2003), sec. 301.

3. The United Kingdom's Higgs Report recently recommended that a minimum of half the board (excluding its chairman) should be independent (para. 9.5); and that the chairman should be independent as well at the time of his or her appointment (para. 5.8). See Derek Higgs, *Review of the Role and Effectiveness of Non-Executive Directors* (the "Higgs Report") (London: Department of Trade and Industry, 2003).

4. Government Commission, "German Corporate Governance Code," 26 February 2002, available at <http://www.ccgi.org/codes/country_documents/germany/corgov_endfassung_e.pdf> (accessed 11 May 2003), para. 5.5.

5. See George P. Baker, Michael C. Jensen, and Kevin J. Murphy, "Compensation and Incentives: Practice versus Theory," *Journal of Finance* 43, no. 3 (1988): 593–616; Michael C. Jensen and Kevin J. Murphy, "Performance Pay and Top-Management Incentives," *Journal of Political Economy* 98, no. 2 (1990): 225–284; and Michael C.

Jensen and Kevin J. Murphy, "CEO Incentives: It's Not How Much You Pay, But How," *Harvard Business Review,* May–June 1990, 138–153.

6. Governance practices in countries outside the United States have been opposed to the use of stock options for outside directors, but the pressure for change is evident. For example, most of the larger Australian companies now require their outside directors to take a portion of their remuneration (usually around 25 percent) in the form of stock— a move designed to demonstrate shareholder "alignment" in their board practices.

7. See Jay W. Lorsch and Elizabeth MacIver, *Pawns or Potentates: The Reality of America's Corporate Boards* (Boston: Harvard Business School Press, 1989), 26–30.

8. William Allen, "Redefining the Role of Outside Directors in an Age of Global Competition" (speech given to the Corporate Securities Law Institute, Northwestern University, Chicago, 30 April 1992).

9. The financial economists referenced in note 5 led the way, but others soon followed. In the words of one observer, "We are all Henry Kravis now," referring to a leading practitioner of the leveraged buyout during the 1980s. The suggestion was that the then-rampant hostile takeovers and leveraged buyouts were no longer needed to force corporate management to maximize shareholder value; the pressure from institutional shareholders and CEOs' own incentives from equity-based compensation more than sufficed. Steven N. Kaplan, "The Evolution of U.S. Corporate Governance: We Are All Henry Kravis Now," unpublished paper, 1997. The Business Roundtable, an association of CEOs of major firms, eventually acknowledged that "the paramount duty of management and of boards of directors is to the corporation's stockholders; the interests of other stakeholders are relevant as a derivative of the duty to stockholders." The Business Roundtable, *Statement on Corporate Governance* (Washington, DC: The Business Roundtable, 1997), 3.

10. Lorsch and MacIver, *Pawns or Potentates,* 37–54.

11. Guhan Subramanian, "The Influence of Antitakeover Statutes on Incorporation Choice: Evidence on the 'Race' Debate and Antitakeover Overreaching," *University of Pennsylvania Law Review* 150, no. 6 (2002): 1795–1873, 1827.

12. In its recent report, the Conference Board cited data from the Bogle Financial Markets Research Center, indicating that in recent years mutual funds have had greater than 100 percent annual turnover in their share holdings, up dramatically from only 15 to 20 percent in the early 1960s. The Conference Board Commission on Public Trust and Private Enterprise, *Corporate Governance: Principles, Recommendations and Specific Best Practice Suggestions* (New York: The Conference Board, 2003), 19.

Chapter Four

1. See Ad Hoc Task Force on Corporate Governance, *OECD Principles of Corporate Governance* (Paris: Organisation for Economic Co-Operation and Development, 1999). The OECD Principles have been embraced by the World Bank.

2. For example, the specific legal requirements with which U.K. boards must comply are very limited. See Jonathan Charkham, *Keeping Good Company: A Study of Corporate Governance in Five Countries* (Oxford: Oxford University Press, 1995), 262. U.S. boards similarly have a great deal of discretion as to structure and role under applicable state law.

3. See Section 141 (a) of the Delaware General Corporation Law, Delaware Code Annotated Title 8, available at <http://www.delcode.state.de.us> (accessed 16 May 2003).

4. Ada Demb and F.-Friedrich Neubauer introduced these archetypes in *The Corporate Board: Confronting the Paradoxes* (New York: Oxford University Press, 1992), 55.

5. William T. Allen, "Free Markets Focus on Corporate Governance," *Directorship*, January 1999, 11.

6. Federal Document Clearing House, "Statement of Dr. Robert K. Jaedicke Before the Permanent Subcommittee on Investigations," The Committee on Senate Governmental Affairs (7 May 2002).

7. As noted earlier, according to one survey, directors of North American companies spend fewer than one hundred hours annually on each board. Egon Zehnder International, *Board of Directors Global Study* (London: Egon Zehnder International, 2000), 52.

8. Learson was closely identified with IBM's highly successful System/360 mainframe project, "a huge gamble even for a firm of IBM's size." D. Quinn Mills and G. Bruce Friesen, *Broken Promises: An Unconventional View of What Went Wrong at IBM* (Boston: Harvard Business School Press, 1996).

9. See, for example, Robert A. G. Monks and Nell Minow, *Corporate Governance* (Oxford: Blackwell Publishers, 2d ed., 2001). This view strongly emphasizes the desirability of the board as an arm's-length monitor of management.

10. For more information on the role of the Medtronic board, see Jay W. Lorsch and Norman Spaulding, "Medtronic, Inc. (A)," Case 9-494-096 (Boston: Harvard Business School, 1994); and Jay W. Lorsch and Katharina Pick, "Medtronic, Inc. (B)," Case 9-400-042 (Boston: Harvard Business School, 1999).

Chapter Five

1. The principal changes proposed for boards were annual elections of all directors, a limit of two "inside" directors per board, a designated "lead director," fully independent committees, and a limit of three boards per director. John Byrne, "How to Fix Corporate Governance," *BusinessWeek*, 6 May 2002, 69–78.

2. See, for example, J. Richard Hackman, *Leading Teams: Setting the Stage for Great Performances* (Boston: Harvard Business School Press, 2002), 116–122; and Jay A. Conger, Edward E. Lawler III, and David L. Finegold, *Corporate Boards: New Strategies for Adding Value at the Top* (San Francisco: Jossey-Bass, 2001), 54–55.

3. For example, in the United States, these three committees are now required by the stock exchanges together with the Securities and Exchange Commission. Governance committees were formerly labeled nominating committees (and still carry this name in many other countries). At a minimum, their purpose is to identify candidates for nomination to the board. Further, they are responsible for approving board members for renomination, and also for overseeing the board's functioning.

4. The question of skill mix is more fully discussed in chapter 6.

5. We are assuming an average committee size of three directors. We discuss our reasons for this later in the chapter.

6. Spencer Stuart, *Spencer Stuart Board Index* 2000 (Chicago: Spencer Stuart: 2000), 8. See also, Korn/Ferry International, *28th Annual Board of Directors Study* 2001 (Los Angeles: Korn/Ferry International, 2001), 10.

7. Egon Zehnder International, *Board of Directors Global Study* (London: Egon Zehnder International, 2000), 28. See also, Heidrick & Struggles, *Is Your Board Fit for the Global Challenge? Corporate Governance in Europe* (London: Heidrick & Struggles International, 2003), 8.

8. Heidrick & Struggles, *Is Your Board Fit for the Global Challenge?*, 8.

9. Egon Zehnder International, *Board of Directors Global Study*, 28.

10. *Spencer Stuart Board Index* 2000, 6.

11. The term "board" is used in the European "dual board structure" countries to describe both supervisory and management boards. Management boards consist entirely of executives, and we regard them as similar to executive committees in other countries. Accordingly, our discussion concerns supervisory boards, which, like the boards in English-speaking countries, are at the top of the governance structure, and which exclude managers from membership.

12. The Higgs Report in 2003 recommended that "at least half the members of the board, excluding the chairman, should be independent non-executive directors." Derek Higgs, *Review of the Role and Effectiveness of Non-Executive Directors* (the "Higgs Report") (London: Department of Trade and Industry, 2003), para. 9.5. The Higgs Report found that the average U.K. listed company had a board comprised of three executive directors, three non-executive directors, and a chairman; while the average FTSE 100 board had twelve directors, including six non-executives, five executives, and the chairman. Higgs Report, para. 4.9.

13. Australian boards are now mostly non-executive. In Singapore and Hong Kong, boards of the larger public companies now have a majority of outside directors. In South Korea, the government has legislated that independent, outside directors must comprise at least one half of the board of larger companies, such as the chaebols, the name given to large Korean conglomerates. See Bernard Black, Barry Metzger, Timothy O'Brien, and Young Moo Shin, "Corporate Governance in Korea at the Millennium: Enhancing International Competitiveness—Final Report and Legal Reform Recommendations to the Ministry of Justice of the Republic of Korea 15 May 2000," *Journal of Corporation Law* 26, no. 3 (2001): 537–608. In Japan, some big companies like Sony are heading in the same direction—a massive change to the long established practice of appointing executives only. Other Asian countries are adopting this trend, but in some cases the "independent directors" are seen as highly influenced by the family interests controlling their companies.

14. Quoted in Margot Sayville, "Ray's Lieutenant Knew How to Keep the Peace," *The Sydney Morning Herald*, 31 August 2002, 47.

15. We do believe executives should be invited to participate in much of the board's work, whether or not they do so as directors of the company. We expand on this in chapter 7.

16. For example, in the United Kingdom in 2002, twenty-four of the FTSE 100 chairmen were formerly the chief executive of the same company. See Higgs Report, 18.

17. General Motors Board of Directors, *GM Board Guidelines on Significant Corporate Governance Issues* (New York: General Motors, 1994), paras. 19 and 20.

18. The Higgs Report proposed that in the United Kingdom non-executive directors who are material shareholders or who represent a significant shareholder should not be classified as independent. Higgs Report, 37.

19. See, for example, The Committee on the Financial Aspects of Corporate Governance, *Report of the Committee on the Financial Aspects of Corporate Governance* (the "Cadbury Report") (London: Gee and Co. Ltd., 1992), para. 4.9; the Higgs Report, para. 5.3; and the Conference Board Commission on Public Trust and Private Enterprise, *Corporate Governance: Principles, Recommendations and Specific Best Practice Suggestions* (New York: The Conference Board, 2003), 7–9.

20. See summarized survey results of McKinsey & Company, "Director Opinion Survey 2002," available at <http://www.mckinsey.com/practices/CorporateGovernance/Research> (accessed 14 May 2003).

21. See Andargachew S. Zelleke, "Freedom and Constraint: The Design of Governance and Leadership Structures in British and American firms," (unpublished Ph.D. diss., Harvard University 2003, chapter 8).

22. Korn/Ferry International, *28th Annual Board of Directors Study 2001*, 19. In the United States most companies that separate the jobs do so as part of their top management succession. The retiring CEO retains the chairman title for a short period while the new CEO takes over the reins.

23. See Rachel E. Silverman, "GE Makes Changes in Board Policy," *Wall Street Journal*, 8 November 2002.

24. In its proposed rules, the New York Stock Exchange has chosen to use the term "presiding director" for this position, which may be a more accurate designation in some boards than "lead director." See New York Stock Exchange, "Corporate Governance Rule Proposals," 1 August 2002, available at <http://www.nyse.com/pdfs/corp_gov_pro_b.pdf> (accessed 16 May 2003), as amended by Amendment No. 1, 4 April 2003, available at <http://www.nyse.com/pdfs/amend1-04-09-03.pdf> (accessed 16 May 2003), subsec. 3.

25. These committees are required in the United States under the proposed rules of the various stock exchanges. Audit committees are also required under Section 301 of the Sarbanes-Oxley Act of 2002, Public Law 107-204, 107th Congress, enacted 30 July 2002 (the "Sarbanes-Oxley Act"), available at <http://news.findlaw.com/hdocs/docs/gwbush/sarbanesoxley072302.pdf> (accessed 13 May 2003).

26. Virtually all North American boards now have audit and compensation committees and, according to one survey, most have nominating and executive committees as well. See Egon Zehnder International, *Board of Directors Global Study*, 42. In Europe, according to another survey, around three-fourths of companies have audit and remuneration committees. Other committees that appear less frequently include executive, strategy, finance, and succession planning. The average European board has 2.6 committees. See Heidrick & Struggles, *Is Your Board Fit for the Global Challenge?*, 11.

27. See New York Stock Exchange, "Corporate Governance Rule Proposals"; NASDAQ, "Summary of NASDAQ Corporate Governance Proposals," 26 February 2003, available at <http://www.nasdaq.com/about/Web_Corp_Gov_Summary%20Feb-revised.pdf> (accessed 16 May 2003); American Stock Exchange, "Enhanced Corporate

Governance—Text of Proposed Rule Changes," 16 May 2003, available at <http://www.amex.com> (accessed 16 May 2003).

28. See, especially, Sarbanes-Oxley Act, sec. 301; New York Stock Exchange, "Corporate Governance Rule Proposals," subsec. 7.

29. See Jay W. Lorsch and Alison H. Watson, "Lukens Inc.: The Melters' Committee, (A)," Case 9-493-070 (Boston: Harvard Business School, 1993).

30. William T. Allen, "Independent Directors in MBO Transactions: Are They Fact or Fantasy?," *The Business Lawyer,* August 1990, 2055–2063.

Chapter Six

1. In this chapter we will discuss the board's role in shaping its membership. Technically, directors can only recommend board members to shareholders for election. But since in most instances the shareholders simply ratify the board's slate, it is in reality the directors who determine the board's membership.

2. As it does in supervisory boards in most countries with dual board structures.

3. Many capable executives don't get to be the CEO but may have run large businesses that are part of major companies. On our board, they will complement the CEOs' experience in running a business. In fact, they may be more useful than the CEOs when dealing with business strategy because they will have been closer to strategic issues in their divisions than someone who has spent most of the past decade in the corporate center.

4. Spencer Stuart, *Spencer Stuart Board Index* 2002 (Chicago: Spencer Stuart: 2002), 8.

5. According to one global survey, only 14 percent of boards had asked a director to resign in the previous two years. Egon Zehnder International, *Board of Directors Global Study* (London: Egon Zehnder International, 2000), 53. Another survey reported that only 24 percent of U.S. boards have ever asked a director to resign or not to stand for reelection because of poor performance. Korn/Ferry International, *28th Annual Board of Directors Study* 2001 (Los Angeles: Korn/Ferry International, 2001), 23.

6. Derek Higgs, *Review of the Role and Effectiveness of Non-Executive Directors* (the "Higgs Report") (London: Department of Trade and Industry, 2003), para. 11.19.

7. These are mostly "whole of board" reviews rather than formal evaluations of individual directors. Forty-two percent of respondents to Korn/Ferry's *28th Annual Board of Directors Study* 2001 had instituted formal performance reviews of their board and 19 percent evaluated the individual directors (22–23). The *Spencer Stuart Board Index* 2000 reported similar results, with around 50 percent of respondents evaluating the whole board and around 20 percent evaluating individual directors (7). Egon Zehnder International's *Board of Directors Global Study* reports that 67 percent of North American and 71 percent of Australian companies evaluate their whole boards, but only 19 percent of boards in Europe, 10 percent in Asia, and 5 percent in Latin America do the same (50).

8. Korn/Ferry International, *28th Annual Board of Directors Study* 2001, 23.

9. In any such exceptional circumstances, companies should explain the reasons to shareholders. Higgs Report, para. 12.5. Moreover, the Higgs Report proposed annual reelection for directors serving more than nine years, para. 12.6.

10. See, for example, Robin Sidel, "Board Compensation Becomes Balancing Act," *Wall Street Journal*, 30 August 2002.

11. Higgs Report, para. 12.24.

12. Joseph B. Treaster, "Directors' Compensation: Cash Laughs Last," *Corporate Board Member*, January–February 2002, 61.

13. As noted earlier, a global study by one search firm reported that North American directors spent eighty-two hours a year on each board. Egon Zehnder International, *Board of Directors Global Study*, 52. Another search firm's survey of U.S. boards reported 156 hours per board in 2001 and 183 hours in 2002 surveys, but these figures included travel time to meetings. Korn/Ferry International, *28th Annual Board of Directors Study 2001*, 18, and *29th Annual Board of Directors Study 2002: Fortune 1000 Highlights* (Los Angeles: Korn/Ferry International, 2002), 14.

14. *Spencer Stuart Board Index 2002*, 17.

15. John M. Nash, President emeritus of the National Association of Corporate Directors, quoted in Treaster, 67.

16. Charles Elson, Director of the Center for Corporate Governance at the University of Delaware, quoted in Treaster, 61.

17. See William M. Mercer Inc. data cited in Treaster, "Directors' Compensation;" *Spencer Stuart Board Index 2002*, 17; Korn/Ferry International, *28th Annual Board of Directors Study 2001*, 17.

18. See Jay W. Lorsch and Elizabeth MacIver, *Pawns or Potentates: The Reality of America's Corporate Boards* (Boston: Harvard Business School Press, 1989), 26–30.

19. For example, the Higgs Report in the United Kingdom expressed opposition to options for non-executive directors, para. 12.27.

Chapter Seven

1. A recent Spencer Stuart survey reports that the average for S&P 500 boards is 7.5 meetings, down from 8.2 the prior year; but a small number of boards have as few as 3 meetings, and 12 percent of boards have at least 11 meetings. Spencer Stuart, *Spencer Stuart Board Index 2002* (Chicago: Spencer Stuart: 2002), 11. Even within an industry there are large variations, for example among banks in 2002: Wells Fargo and State Street (6 meetings); US Bancorp and Northern Trust (7 meetings); Fleet Boston (8 meetings); and JP Morgan Chase and Citigroup (10 meetings).

2. Heidrick & Struggles, *Is Your Board Fit for the Global Challenge? Corporate Governance in Europe* (London: Heidrick & Struggles International, 2003), 9.

3. *Spencer Stuart Board Index 2002*, 11; and Heidrick & Struggles, *Is Your Board Fit for the Global Challenge?*, 9.

4. These would include BHP Billiton, Brambles, AMP, and Commonwealth Bank of Australia. In several of these, spreading their business into the Northern Hemisphere has precipitated the change—as they try to attract overseas directors, and because monthly meetings become very difficult when management spends so much time traveling.

5. For an elaboration of this set of tools, see Robert S. Kaplan and David P. Norton, *The Balanced Scorecard: Translating Strategy into Action* (Boston: Harvard Business School Press, 1996).

Chapter Eight

1. See New York Stock Exchange, "Corporate Governance Rule Proposals," 1 August 2002, available at <http://www.nyse.com/pdfs/corp_gov_pro_b.pdf> (accessed 16 May 2003), as amended by Amendment No. 1, 4 April 2003, available at <http://www.nyse.com/pdfs/amend1-04-09-03.pdf> (accessed 16 May 2003), subsec. 3.

Chapter Nine

1. B. George, *Authentic Leadership* (San Francisco: Jossey-Bass, 2003), 172.

2. We feel this is especially important in the United States for audit committees since Sarbanes-Oxley has given them so much power independent of the board as a whole. See Sarbanes-Oxley Act of 2002, Public Law 107-204, 107th Congress, enacted 30 July 2002 (the "Sarbanes-Oxley Act"), available at <http://news.findlaw.com/hdocs/docs/gwbush/sarbanesoxley072302.pdf> (accessed 13 May 2003), sec. 301.

3. Over a decade ago, Professor Michael Jensen applauded "the eclipse of the large public corporation" by newer types of organizations in many sectors of the U.S. economy (73). He observed the rising importance of corporate structures with no public shareholders, such as companies taken private in leveraged buyout transactions. Such structures were overseen by "active investors" rather than corporate boards (65). Going further, Jensen argued that "The idea that outside directors with little or no equity stake in the company could effectively monitor and discipline the managers who selected them has proven hollow at best" (64). In his view, the new corporate structures overcame the central weakness of the public corporation—the inherent conflict between owners and managers over the control and use of corporate resources—and were demonstrably more efficient, effective, and value creating. Michael C. Jensen, "Eclipse of the Public Corporation," *Harvard Business Review,* September–October 1989, 61–74.

4. See Rafael La Porta, Florencio Lopez-de-Silanes, and Andrei Shleifer, "Corporate Ownership Around the World," *Journal of Finance* 54, no. 2 (1999): 471–517.

5. In his farewell speech in 2002, Lord Young, the retiring head of the United Kingdom's Institute of Directors, argued that boards full of independent directors are a waste of time. "We have spent more time and effort on corporate governance over the past decade than we have ever done since the birth of the limited liability company. But the only result of all this well-meaning, but I believe misguided, effort is that we are more concerned about corporate governance than ever before. The biggest—the most dangerous—nonsense is the role that we expect non-executive directors to perform. . . . All they can do at best is judge what management tells them. If management is not too forthcoming, they can never even know, until it is far too late. . . . Can they ever know the business as well as the executives? No, they can't. In that case, why bother? Why bother with non-execs at all?" For the full text of his remarks, see Lord Young, *The Business,* 28 April 2002.

Index

About the Authors

COLIN B. CARTER has worked as a management consultant for over twenty-five years, for most of this time as a Senior Vice President of The Boston Consulting Group (BCG) working with CEOs and senior executives on strategy and organization issues.

His particular interest in corporate boards began when he was working as a consultant with senior executives. At the end of the assignments, he often presented his results to the boards of the companies with which he had been working. This led to a larger interest in how boards function and, in particular, how part-time independent directors make sense of their demanding duties. He has spent much of the last decade carrying out board performance reviews for a number of corporations and, inside BCG, Colin has taken worldwide leadership of the topic of corporate boards and advises consultants on board-related issues. These engagements have exposed him to board design and performance issues in many countries around the world. He has also been a speaker on corporate governance and the role of boards at conferences in Europe and Asia.

Colin has taught in graduate management education programs at IMD in Switzerland, Yale University, and the University of Melbourne.

He retired from full-time consulting at BCG in 2000 and is currently retained part-time as an adviser, where he focuses on providing board-related advice to consulting teams as well as carrying out board reviews for his own portfolio of clients. He serves as a director of two publicly listed Australian companies—Wesfarmers and Origin Energy; he is a Commissioner of The Australian Football League and a director of several not-for-profit organizations. A graduate of Melbourne University and Harvard Business School, Colin lives in Melbourne, Australia with his wife Angie. They have three adult sons, Paul, James, and Christopher.

JAY W. LORSCH is the Louis E. Kirstein Professor of Human Relations at Harvard Business School (HBS) and is a leading authority on corporate boards of directors. His focus on corporate boards began with his path-breaking book, *Pawns or Potentates: The Reality of America's Corporate Boards* (1989). Professor Lorsch teaches in and leads educational courses about corporate boards for both M.B.A. students and practicing directors; he also chairs HBS's Global Corporate Governance Initiative.

His current interests also include professional service firms, as reflected in his recent book, *Aligning the Stars: When Professionals Drive Results* (with Thomas Tierney, 2003). He is also the author of numerous articles and fifteen books, including *Organization and Environment*, which won the Academy of Management Book Award and the James A. Hamilton Hospital Administration Book Award. At HBS he was a Senior Associate Dean from 1986 to 1995, responsible first for the faculty's research activities and later for its Executive Education programs.

As a consultant, he has worked on organizational and corporate board-related issues for such companies as Alston & Bird LLP, Applied Materials, the Bank of Montreal, Cinergy, Gillette Company, Goldman Sachs, and Medtronic, Inc. He has also served as a director of a number of public and private companies including Benckiser, Brunswick Corporation, and Computer Associates.

Jay and his wife Patricia live in Cambridge, Massachusetts, and have five adult children.